SPORT FIRST AID CLASSROOM STUDY GUIDE

Fourth Edition

American Sport Education Program

HUMAN KINETICS

Sport First Aid Classroom Study Guide, Fourth Edition

ISBN-10: 0-7360-7602-6
ISBN-13: 978-0-7360-7602-9

Author: Christine M. Drews
Acquisitions Editors: Scott Parker and Patricia Sammann
Managing Editors: Kathleen D. Bernard and Pamela Mazurak
Copyeditor: Pat Connolly
Graphic Designer: Fred Starbird
Graphic Artists: Kim McFarland and Tara Welsch
Cover Designer: Keith Blomberg
Photographer (cover): © Human Kinetics
Art Manager: Kelly Hendren
Illustrator: Mic Greenberg
Printer: Versa Press

Printed in the United States of America   10 9 8 7 6 5 4 3 2 1

HUMAN KINETICS
Web site: www.HumanKinetics.com

United States: Human Kinetics
P.O. Box 5076
Champaign, IL 61825-5076
800-747-4457
e-mail: humank@hkusa.com

Canada: Human Kinetics
475 Devonshire Road Unit 100
Windsor, ON N8Y 2L5
800-465-7301 (in Canada only)
e-mail: info@hkcanada.com

Europe: Human Kinetics
107 Bradford Road
Stanningley
Leeds LS28 6AT, United Kingdom
+44 (0) 113 255 5665
e-mail: hk@hkeurope.com

Australia: Human Kinetics
57A Price Avenue
Lower Mitcham, South Australia 5062
08 8372 0999
e-mail: info@hkaustralia.com

New Zealand: Human Kinetics
Division of Sports Distributors NZ Ltd.
P.O. Box 300 226 Albany
North Shore City
Auckland
0064 9 448 1207
e-mail: info@humankinetics.co.nz

Contents

Preface

Welcome to the Sport First Aid Classroom course! The goal of this course is to help you become an effective first responder when one of your athletes gets injured or becomes ill. The classroom course and self-study activities are designed to help you learn what steps you should take to become confident in responding to your athletes' injuries and illnesses.

The *Sport First Aid Classroom Study Guide* has two sections: classroom units and self-study units. You'll use the classroom units during the classroom course. Follow along in this part of the study guide as your instructor leads you through activities, DVD segments, and discussions. All of the resources you need for the classroom course are in these classroom units, and plenty of space has been left for you to write notes.

After you've completed the classroom course, you'll use the self-study units to learn additional sport first aid information. You'll read the *Sport First Aid* book as you work though these self-study units. Become familiar with the book so that you can refer to it if your athletes become injured or ill. At the end of each self-study unit, you'll find solutions to the activities so that you can check your responses and clarify your understanding.

Attending the classroom course, working through the self-study units, and reading *Sport First Aid* will prepare you for the Sport First Aid Test. Participating fully in the classroom course and diligently studying the self-study units should improve your score on the test and, more important, enhance your ability to be an effective sport first aider for the athletes you coach.

SPORT FIRST AID CLASSROOM UNITS

Introduction to Sport First Aid

(10 minutes)

PURPOSE: To introduce you to the Sport First Aid course, including the course purpose, learning objectives, agenda, and resources.

LEARNING OBJECTIVES

In this unit, you will learn

- the purpose, learning objectives, and agenda for the Sport First Aid course and
- how you might use the course text and study guide.

Unit Overview

Topic	Activities	Time (minutes)
A. Welcome and Introductions	Introductions.	5
B. Overview of the Sport First Aid Course	Learn about the purpose, objectives, and agenda for the course. Discuss housekeeping details (rest rooms and so forth).	3
C. Course Resources	Look at the *Sport First Aid* book and the *Sport First Aid Classroom Study Guide*.	2

UNIT CONTENT

A Welcome and Introductions (5 minutes)

- Be prepared to introduce yourself by giving your
  - name,
  - present position,
  - sports coached, and
  - length of career.

- Your Sport First Aid course package includes the following:
  - The course text, *Sport First Aid, Third Edition*
  - A *Sport First Aid Classroom Study Guide*
  - The Sport First Aid Quick Reference Card
  - A Sport First Aid Classroom Test Package that includes a course evaluation form; a Sport First Aid Test; a test answer form; the instructions for completing the test answer form; a preaddressed envelope in which you will mail the completed test answer form; and a cardboard insert to ensure that the test form is not damaged in the mail.

B Overview of the Sport First Aid Course (3 minutes)

The purpose of the Sport First Aid course is to help you learn the skills you need to be a competent first responder to players' injuries and illnesses. This course has been designed to help you

- develop a basic knowledge of sport injuries and illnesses,
- recognize signs and symptoms of common sport injuries and illnesses,
- administer appropriate sport first aid, and
- learn to use the *Sport First Aid* book as a reference tool.

Sport First Aid Classroom Course Agenda

Unit number	Unit title	Time (minutes)
1	Introduction to Sport First Aid	10
2	Your Role on the Athletic Health Care Team	15
3	Types of Injuries	20
4	Emergency Action Steps and Providing Life Support	50

Sport First Aid Classroom Course Agenda *(continued)*

Unit number	Unit title	Time (minutes)
	BREAK (IN TWO-DAY FORMAT, MAY STOP FIRST DAY HERE.)	10
5	Physical Assessment and Providing Immediate First Aid	60
6	Moving Injured or Sick Athletes	10
7	Closed Head and Spine Injuries	20
8	Musculoskeletal Injuries	35
9	Sport First Aid Wrap-Up	20
	TOTAL TIME:	4 hours (not including breaks)

The Learning Environment

- Feel free to ask questions at any time. There are no dumb questions. Be assertive about what you need to understand sport first aid better.
- Use the study guide in whatever way makes it easier for you to learn. Take notes, make check marks, underline important things—do whatever you need to do to make it a worthwhile resource.
- Relax. Enjoy yourself. Be open. Participate. We're all here to learn together.

Housekeeping Details

- Where to put coats
- Seating arrangements
- Rest room locations
- Refreshments
- Other

C Course Resources (2 minutes)

- *Sport First Aid Classroom Study Guide*
  - You will use the first part of the study guide today.
  - We can't cover everything in this classroom portion of the course, so the second part of the study guide includes self-study exercises that you can do on your own to prepare for the test. It's jam-packed with activities to help you get into the book and learn sport first aid.

- Finally, the study guide includes answers to the self-study activities so that you can check your work.

• *Sport First Aid*

- The first few chapters of the *Sport First Aid* book contain general information for you as a coach and as a first responder in injury and illness situations.
- Chapters 4 and 5 cover the emergency action steps and physical assessment, which we'll be spending a lot of time on during this course.
- Chapter 6 describes how to move an injured or ill athlete.
- Chapters 7 through 15 list injuries and illnesses that you might encounter as a coach, with corresponding symptoms and signs for easier recognition and appropriate first aid steps for you to take.

Your Role on the Athletic Health Care Team

(15 minutes)

> **PURPOSE:** To introduce you to your role in working on the athletic health care team and teach you how to prepare a sport first aid game plan.

LEARNING OBJECTIVES

In this unit, you will learn

- about the athletic health care team and your role on it and
- how to develop a sport first aid game plan.

Unit Overview

Topic	Activities	Time (minutes)
A. Unit Introduction	Hear about the unit's purpose, objectives, and agenda.	1
B. Coach's Role on the Athletic Health Care Team and How to Develop a Sport First Aid Game Plan	Watch a DVD segment, "Your Role on the Athletic Health Care Team."	5
C. Evaluating Your Sport First Aid Game Plan	Fill out Chapter 2 Replay on pages 27 to 28 of *Sport First Aid*.	8
D. Unit Summary	Review key unit points.	1

UNIT CONTENT

A Unit Introduction (1 minute)

- Your role on the athletic health care team and how to prepare a sport first aid game plan
- What you need to do to complete a sport first aid game plan for your particular situation

B Coach's Role on the Athletic Health Care Team and How to Develop a Sport First Aid Game Plan (5 minutes)

On the DVD Segment, "Your Role on the Athletic Health Care Team"

- Legal definitions of your role as a coach
- Parental expectations
- Other members of the athletic health care team
- Playing it safe with return to play, including the importance of treatment and rehabilitation
- How to develop a sport first aid game plan

C Evaluating Your Sport First Aid Game Plan (8 minutes)

Activity 2.1 Evaluating Your Sport First Aid Game Plan

Introduction

You heard on the DVD segment that to be prepared for emergencies, you need to develop a sport first aid game plan. This involves collecting health records of your athletes, creating a weather emergency plan, preparing a medical emergency plan, and so forth.

- For the next few minutes, you'll evaluate what you need to do in your particular coaching situation to complete your sport first aid game plan.
- When you complete the self-study portion of this course, you'll actually complete your own sport first aid game plan.

Resources

- Chapter 2 Replay on pages 27-28 of *Sport First Aid*

Instructions

1. Work in pairs.
2. Talk through the checklist together.
3. Check off the items that you've already accomplished in your particular coaching situation and note the steps that you need to complete.
4. Complete the checklist for your situation only, but discuss each item with your partner. You may gain insights from each other about how to efficiently complete certain parts of the sport first aid game plan.
5. You probably won't get through the entire checklist in the time allotted, and that is all right. Complete as much of the checklist as you can now, and then you can finish it on your own later.
6. Take 7 minutes to complete your work.

Activity Outcome

When you're done, you should have completed as much of the checklist as possible. The items that you have already completed in your coaching situation should have a check mark next to them, and you should have a good sense of which steps you still need to take care of.

D Unit Summary (1 minute)

- Along with many other legal duties, you have a legal obligation to provide emergency medical assistance.
- Parents expect you to provide a safe environment for their children. They expect you to have some knowledge of sport first aid and to know where to refer them for more information.
- You should develop good working relationships with other members of the athletic health care team and support their decisions regarding treatment and rehabilitation.
- Players who are injured or sick can return to play only after all symptoms and signs have subsided or after examination and release by a physician.
- A sport first aid game plan includes gathering health records for each athlete, developing a weather emergency plan, checking facilities for hazards, checking equipment for proper fit and usage, stocking a first aid kit, arranging for preseason physicals and fitness screenings, incorporating

conditioning into your program, and developing a medical emergency plan.

- Use the forms provided in chapter 2 of *Sport First Aid* to guide you in preparing for emergencies.

Types of Injuries

(20 minutes)

PURPOSE: To help you learn how to recognize the main types of acute and chronic injuries.

LEARNING OBJECTIVES

In this unit, you will learn

- how most injuries occur,
- what distinguishes acute and chronic injuries, and
- how to recognize the main types of acute and chronic injuries.

Unit Overview

Topic	Activities	Time (minutes)
A. Unit Introduction	Hear about the unit's purpose, objectives, and agenda.	1
B. Types of Injuries and How They Occur	Fill out a table while watching the DVD segment, "Types of Injuries and How They Occur."	9
C. Injury Causes	In teams, complete mechanisms (injury causes) columns in a table. Points will be awarded for correct answers.	9
D. Unit Summary	Review key unit points.	1

UNIT CONTENT

A Unit Introduction (1 minute)

- Causes of injury
- Acute injuries
- Chronic injuries

B Types of Injuries and How They Occur (9 minutes)

Activity 3.1 Types of Injuries

Introduction

Knowing how an injury occurred and whether it occurred suddenly or over time may help you to correctly identify an injury and respond with appropriate first aid care. In this activity, you'll fill out a table as we watch a DVD segment.

Resources

- The table, Examples of Injuries That Affect Specific Body Tissues. (This table is provided on page 11.)

Instructions

1. Work individually.
2. As you watch the DVD segment, listen for
   a. what types of injuries affect different body tissues and
   b. whether an injury is acute or chronic.
3. Fill in the table as you watch the DVD segment.
   a. In the second column, write the types of injuries that can affect each body tissue. For example, you'll hear on the DVD segment that bones can sustain closed fractures, so you would write *Closed fracture* in the second column.
   b. In the third column,
      - write *Acute* if the injury occurs suddenly and is the result of a specific injury mechanism,
      - write *Chronic* if the injury develops over a period of several weeks and is typically caused by repeated injury, or
      - write *Acute or Chronic* if both could be the case.

Examples of Injuries That Affect Specific Body Tissues

Tissue	Injury	Type of injury
Bone	Closed fracture	Acute
Cartilage		
Ligament		
Muscle		
Tendon		
Bursa		
Skin		
Eye		
Other organs (heart, kidney, and so forth)		

For example, bones can sustain closed fractures. Closed fractures occur suddenly, so you would write *Acute* in the third column. As you can see, the answers for this injury have been provided in the table as an example.

Activity Outcome

When you're done, you should have completed the "Injury" and "Type of injury" columns in the table. We'll review the results after watching the DVD segment.

C Injury Causes (9 minutes)

Activity 3.2 Injury Causes

Introduction

As explained on the DVD segment, injuries are usually caused by one of three mechanisms: compression, tension, or shearing. In this activity, you'll learn what mechanisms often cause which injuries.

Resources

- The table, Injuries and Their Mechanisms. (This table is provided on page 13.)

Instructions

1. Work in teams of four if possible.
2. Work with your team to decide which mechanisms can cause each injury listed in the table.
3. Place an *X* in the column if that mechanism can cause the injury. For instance, if compression can cause a contusion, place an *X* under *Compression* and across from *Contusion*.
4. You may place more than one *X* in a row. That is, some injuries can be caused by several different mechanisms, and you should place an *X* under each of those. Other injuries may be caused by only one mechanism.
5. You will have 6 minutes to complete the table. You'll need to work quickly.
6. At the end, we will award points for correct answers and see which team won the challenge.

Activity Outcome

When you're done, you should have completed the table with *Xs* in the columns that match the injuries with their mechanisms.

Injuries and Their Mechanisms

Acute Injuries	Compression	Tension	Shearing
Contusions			
Abrasions			
Lacerations			
Incisions			
Sprains			
Acute strains			
Cartilage tears			
Dislocations and subluxations			
Bone fractures			
Epiphyseal fractures			
Chronic Injuries			
Bursitis			
Tendinosis, tenosynovitis, and paratendinitis			
Stress fractures			

D Unit Summary (1 minute)

- Injuries are often caused by one of three mechanisms: compression, tension, or shearing.
- Injuries can be distinguished by the time it takes for them to develop.
  - Acute injuries occur suddenly as a result of a specific injury mechanism.
  - Chronic injuries develop over a period of several weeks and are typically caused by repeated injury.
- Knowing which mechanism caused an injury and knowing whether the injury occurred suddenly or over time may help you to correctly identify an injury and respond with appropriate first aid care.

Unit 3 Activity Outcomes

Examples of Injuries That Affect Specific Body Tissues—Activity 3.1 Outcome

Tissue	Injury	Type of injury
Bone	Closed fracture Open fracture Avulsion fracture Osteoarthritis Stress fracture	Acute Acute Acute or chronic Chronic Chronic
Cartilage	Tear Contusion	Acute or chronic Acute
Ligament	Sprain	Acute
Muscle	Strain	Acute or chronic
Tendon	Strain Tenosynovitis Tendinosis Paratendinitis	Acute Chronic Chronic Chronic
Bursa	Bursitis Contusion	Chronic Acute
Skin	Laceration Incision Abrasion Puncture Avulsion (example: ear lobe)	Acute Acute Acute Acute Acute
Eye	Puncture Abrasion (corneal)	Acute Acute
Other organs (heart, kidney, and so forth)	Puncture Contusion	Acute Acute

Injuries and Their Mechanisms—Activity 3.2 Outcome

Acute injuries	Compression	Tension	Shearing
Contusions	X		
Abrasions			X
Lacerations	X		X
Incisions	X		
Sprains		X	X
Acute strains		X	
Cartilage tears	X		X
Dislocations and subluxations	X	X	
Bone fractures	X		
Epiphyseal fractures	X	X	
Chronic injuries			
Bursitis	X	X	X
Tendinosis, tenosynovitis, and paratendinitis		X	
Stress fractures	X		

Emergency Action Steps and Providing Life Support

(50 minutes)

PURPOSE: To help you learn how to perform the emergency action steps and provide life support.

LEARNING OBJECTIVES

In this unit, you will learn

- how to perform the emergency action steps,
- how to recognize and respond to an airway blockage,
- what to do if an athlete stops breathing, and
- why learning CPR and AED is critical for a coach.

Unit Overview

Topic	Activities	Time (minutes)
A. Unit Introduction	Hear about the unit's purpose, objectives, and agenda.	1
B. Performing the Emergency Action Steps for a Responsive Athlete	Watch a DVD segment, "Performing the Emergency Action Steps." In groups of three, practice checking a responsive athlete's airway, breathing, and circulation.	18
C. Performing the Emergency Action Steps for an Unresponsive Athlete	In pairs, practice checking an unresponsive athlete's breathing and circulation and practice opening an airway.	15

(continued)

Unit Overview *(continued)*

Topic	Activities	Time (minutes)
D. Maintaining Life Support	Watch a DVD segment, "Maintaining Life Support." In teams, practice first aid for airway obstructions in responsive athletes, including the Heimlich maneuver.	14
E. Unit Summary	Review key unit points.	2

UNIT CONTENT

A Unit Introduction (1 minute)

- How to perform the emergency action steps for a responsive athlete
- How to perform the emergency action steps for an unresponsive athlete
- How to recognize and respond to an airway obstruction

B Performing the Emergency Action Steps for a Responsive Athlete (18 minutes)

On the DVD Segment, "Performing the Emergency Action Steps"

- Assessing the scene and the athlete
- Alerting EMS (or emergency action plan)
- Attending to the athlete's ABCs

Activity 4.1 Performing the Emergency Action Steps for a Responsive Athlete

Introduction

You heard on the DVD segment what the emergency action steps are. In this activity you'll practice following those steps for a responsive athlete. To complete the activity, you'll need to know a little about first aid for a lower leg fracture. This and other illnesses and injuries are covered in the *Sport First Aid* book.

The *Sport First Aid* book includes a reference guide for over 110 sport injuries and illnesses. The description of most of these injuries and illnesses begins with four sections that will help you identify the injury or illness. These sections are as follows:

- Definition
- Causes
- Ask if Experiencing Symptoms
- Check for Signs

Resources

- The Athlete, Coach, and Observer Scenarios. (These are provided after the following instructions and activity outcome.)
- Chapter 13 in *Sport First Aid*

Instructions

1. Work in groups of three. One person will be the athlete, one person will be the coach, and one person will be an observer.
2. When the activity starts, do the following:
   a. Select which role each of you will play.
   b. Spend a minute preparing for your roles.
      - If you're the athlete, read through the Athlete Scenario (see below) and be prepared to respond appropriately.
      - If you're the coach, read through the Coach Scenario (see page 18). You should also have chapter 13 of *Sport First Aid* open to refer to.
      - If you're the observer, read through the Observer Scenario (see pages 18 and 19), which you will use to evaluate the role play.
3. Start the role play.
4. After completing the role play, discuss with your group the first aid steps that you would take.
5. You'll have 8 minutes to complete this activity.

Activity Outcome

When you're done, your group should have completed one role play. You will have practiced performing the emergency action steps for a responsive athlete.

▶ *Athlete Scenario* -

You're a gymnast who's fallen off a balance beam and broken your leg. Your leg hurts, and you heard a "pop" when you landed. There is swelling in the leg, and the leg's skin color is somewhat bluish. You try to move a bit when the coach arrives.

▶ Coach Scenario -

You're supervising a gymnastics workout when you see one of your athletes fall off the balance beam with a "thud." She is lying on the floor and grimacing in pain, and you see her teammates gathering around her.

To take the emergency action steps, do the following:

1. Assess the scene.
2. Assess the athlete.
3. Alert EMS or your emergency action plan.
4. Attend to the athlete.

Say out loud what you're doing as you do it.

▶ Observer Scenario -

Your role is to evaluate if the coach took the correct actions for each step. Use the following checklist to check off items the coach completes.

ASSESSING THE SCENE

☐ Move all other players and bystanders away.

☐ Consider if the environment is safe. Do you need to move the ill or injured athlete because conditions are dangerous?

☐ Calm the athlete and keep him or her from moving.

☐ Consider if you need to roll the athlete over or remove equipment in order to evaluate his or her condition or provide first aid.

ASSESS THE ATHLETE

☐ Review in your mind how the injury or illness occurred.

☐ Review in your mind the athlete's medical history, if you know it.

☐ Check the responsiveness of the athlete by gently tapping or squeezing his or her shoulder and by asking "Are you all right, (athlete's name)?"

ALERT EMS

☐ If your assessment indicates a condition that requires medical attention, have someone call 9-1-1 or activate your emergency action plan.

ATTEND TO THE ATHLETE

- ☐ Identify yourself (if the athlete doesn't know you) and ask the athlete's permission to help.
- ☐ Make sure the athlete is fully responsive and is breathing normally (if not, begin CPR).
- ☐ Look for and control any severe bleeding with direct pressure.
- ☐ Look for normal tissue color and body temperature.
- ☐ While waiting for medical assistance, continue to attend to the ABCs and control bleeding and monitor tissue color and body temperature.
- ☐ Help the athlete maintain normal body temperature and, if it's available and you're properly trained, give the athlete emergency oxygen.

C Emergency Action Steps for an Unresponsive Athlete (15 minutes)

Activity 4.2 Emergency Action Steps for an Unresponsive Athlete

Introduction

As you just practiced, once you've established it is safe to treat the athlete, you should check the athlete's ABCs—airway, breathing, and circulation. In this activity, you'll practice checking an *unresponsive* athlete's breathing and circulation and practice opening an unresponsive athlete's airway.

To complete the activity, you'll use the Sport First Aid Quick Reference Card included in your course package.

Sport First Aid Quick Reference Card

Remember that the Sport First Aid Quick Reference Card is two-sided: One side illustrates the emergency action steps, and the other side illustrates the physical assessment. The side with the emergency action steps is a one-stop guide to conducting those steps, whether the athlete is responsive or unresponsive. It includes steps you should follow to

- determine if the athlete is responsive;
- check airway, breathing, and circulation; and
- follow up with appropriate first aid care.

Resources

- The Emergency Action Steps for an Unresponsive Athlete Scenario (provided after the following instructions and activity outcome)
- The emergency action steps side of the Sport First Aid Quick Reference Card

Instructions

1. Work in pairs.
2. First review the Emergency Action Steps for an Unresponsive Athlete Scenario, and then follow the steps in the scenario, using the Sport First Aid Quick Reference Card to guide what you do.

   a. One partner plays the role of a soccer player who has collapsed on the field. The athlete is unresponsive. This person should lie on his or her back and breathe normally.

   b. The other partner plays the role of the coach and performs the emergency action steps, using the steps outlined on the Sport First Aid Quick Reference Card.

3. When the coach has completed the emergency action steps, reverse roles and repeat the entire scenario so that both partners have a chance to practice all skills.
4. You'll have 10 minutes to complete this activity, with each person in the coach's role for 5 minutes.

Activity Outcome

When you're done, you should have practiced checking breathing, opening an airway, and checking the circulation of an unresponsive athlete.

▶ Emergency Action Steps for an Unresponsive Athlete Scenario - - - - - -

In the second inning, your softball team has just made a play, but you now notice that several players are standing around one of your team members, who's lying face up on the ground. You run out to check if she's responsive, but she is not. None of the players knows exactly what happened.

1. Take initial first aid steps.

   a. Check for response.

   - Coach: Tap the athlete on the shoulder and ask "Are you all right, (athlete's name)?"

   Athlete: Do not respond.

b. Send helper to call 911.

- Since no helper is present in this role play, pretend to send someone.
- Tell the helper to provide information regarding the location and address, type of injury, and the first aid being administered.

2. Check the athlete's airway and breathing.

a. Look, listen, and feel for 5, but no more than 10, seconds.

3. Assume you are unable to detect the athlete breathing. Practice opening an unresponsive athlete's airway. Use the head tilt/chin lift method to open the airway.

4. Pretend that an open airway has been established—the athlete is breathing. Check the athlete's skin color and body temperature to see if circulation has been restricted.

5. Reverse roles and repeat the entire activity so that both partners have a chance to practice all skills.

D Maintaining Life Support (14 minutes)

On the DVD Segment, "Maintaining Life Support"

- How to recognize and respond to an airway blockage
  - Mild and severe airway blockage in a responsive athlete (includes performing the Heimlich maneuver)
  - Severe airway blockage in an unresponsive athlete
- What to do if an athlete is in cardiac arrest

Activity 4.3 Airway Blockage in a Responsive Athlete

Introduction

During this activity, you'll practice providing first aid care for severe airway blockage in a responsive athlete.

Resources

- The Airway Blockage Scenario (provided after the following instructions and activity outcome)

Instructions

1. Work in pairs.

2. Read the introduction to the Airway Blockage Scenario, and then follow the numbered instructions.

3. One person will play the role of the athlete; the other person will play the role of the coach who is responding to the situation.

4. When the coach has responded to the severe airway blockage, reverse roles and repeat the entire scenario so that both partners have a chance to practice all skills.

5. You'll have 8 minutes to complete this activity, with each person in the coach's role for 4 minutes.

Activity Outcome

When you're done, you should have practiced providing first aid care (including the Heimlich maneuver) for severe airway blockage in a responsive athlete.

▶ Airway Obstruction Scenario -

A basketball player (your partner) is grasping his or her throat, giving the universal choking sign. The athlete is coughing and gasping. The athlete had been chewing gum. You provide first aid care for this athlete, who has a *mild airway blockage*, and this is what happens:

• You ask, "Are you okay?" The athlete says "yes" but has trouble breathing and gives the universal choking sign.

• You encourage the athlete to cough.

• You monitor the athlete, hoping the object will be dislodged and the athlete will begin to breathe normally.

Unfortunately, the basketball player's situation gets worse. The athlete still exhibits the universal choking sign, but the airway becomes severely blocked, and the athlete is unable to cough or speak. Provide first aid care for this athlete, who now has a *total airway blockage*.

1. Coach: Ask, "Are you choking?"

   Athlete: Shake your head "yes," or give the universal choking signal.

2. Coach: Ask, "Can I help?"

   Athlete: Shake your head "yes."

3. Coach: Begin the Heimlich maneuver. Practice the correct hand position and placement, *but only simulate the thrusts rather than actually performing them fully.*

   a. Stand behind the athlete, if an adult, and kneel if a child.

    b. Make a fist. Place the thumb side against the athlete's abdomen, just above the navel (see figure 4.10, page 59 in *Sport First Aid*

    c. Give quick inward and upward thrusts.

    d. Continue the compressions until

        1. the object is expelled; or

        2. the athlete loses responsiveness from lack of air, then do CPR.

Athlete: Pretend your gum is dislodged and you're able to start breathing again.

    4. Reverse roles and repeat the entire activity so that both partners have a chance to practice all skills.

The Heimlich Maneuver

- As discussed in the *Sport First Aid* book, it's very important to use the correct hand position and placement for the Heimlich maneuver.
- The Heimlich maneuver should not be performed on infants under 1.
- Only health care providers should perform the Heimlich maneuver on unresponsive victims.
- If the athlete is choking but shakes his or her head "no" when you ask if you can help, send for emergency medical assistance and assess for other causes of the breathing difficulties. These are discussed in chapter 7 of *Sport First Aid.*

E Unit Summary (2 minutes)

- When an athlete goes down due to an injury or illness, the first thing you should do is quickly assess the scene and the athlete.
- After quickly assessing the scene and the athlete, and alerting EMS if necessary, attend to the athlete's ABCs of airway, breathing, and circulation. Attending to the ABCs is done differently depending on whether the athlete is responsive or unresponsive.
- Maintaining the ABCs (airway, breathing, and circulation) is the top priority.
- The first aid care that you provide will differ if the airway is mildly blocked versus severely blocked and if the athlete is responsive or unresponsive.
- If an athlete is not breathing, begin CPR.
- If you were to witness a sudden collapse of an adult, you would provide compressions-only CPR, rather than rescue breathing and compressions.

- Cardiac arrest occurs when an athlete stops breathing and the athlete's heart stops beating.
- All coaches should become CPR and AED certified. Become certified by taking the ASEP course *CPR/AED for Coaches* or by attending certification classes offered by the following agencies: American Safety and Health Institute, American Red Cross, American Heart Association, or National Safety Council.

Unit 4 Activity Outcomes

► **Emergency Action Steps for a Responsive Athlete—Activity 4.1 Outcome** - - - - - - - - - - - - - -

ASSESS THE SCENE

1. The coach moves all the teammates away.
2. The coach considers if the environment is safe and whether to move the athlete.
3. The coach calms the athlete and keeps her from moving.
4. The coach considers whether there's a need to move or roll the athlete over.

ASSESS THE ATHLETE

1. The coach reviews in his or her mind how the injury occurred.
2. The coach reviews in his or her mind the athlete's medical history.
3. The coach checks the athlete's responsiveness by asking "Are you all right, (athlete's name)?"

   (Tapping the shoulder isn't necessary, since the athlete is obviously moving.)

ALERT

It appears that the athlete's leg is badly hurt, so the coach either calls EMS (9-1-1) or sends an assistant to do so.

ATTEND TO THE ABCS

1. The coach asks the athlete's permission to help.
2. The coach checks to make sure the athlete is fully responsive and is breathing normally.
3. The coach looks for any severe bleeding.
4. The coach looks at the athlete's tissue color and body temperature.
5. While waiting for medical assistance, the coach continues to attend to the athlete's ABCs and monitors her tissue color and body temperature (in case of shock).
6. The coach helps the athlete maintain normal body temperature by covering her with a blanket. He or she also gives her emergency oxygen (if the coach is trained in its use and it is available).

Physical Assessment and Providing Immediate First Aid

(60 minutes)

PURPOSE: To help you learn how to conduct a physical assessment, control bleeding, minimize shock, splint unstable injuries, and respond to heat-related illnesses.

LEARNING OBJECTIVES

In this unit, you will learn

- how to perform a physical assessment of an injured or ill athlete,
- how to control arterial and venous (profuse) bleeding and capillary (slow, steady) bleeding,
- what methods to use in minimizing shock,
- how to splint unstable injuries,
- how to use the PRICE method to minimize local tissue damage, and
- how to respond to heat-related illnesses.

Unit Overview

Topic	Activities	Time (minutes)
A. Unit Introduction	Hear about the unit's purpose, objectives, and agenda.	1
B. Physical Assessment	Watch a DVD segment, "Physical Assessment: History, Inspection, and Touch."	7
C. Controlling Bleeding and Protecting Against Blood Borne Pathogens	Watch a DVD segment, "Controlling Bleeding." Practice three methods of controlling bleeding.	17
D. Controlling Tissue Damage (Shock), Applying Splints, and Applying Compression Wraps	Watch a DVD segment, "Shock, Splints, and Compression Wraps." As a class, practice positioning an ill or injured athlete. In pairs, practice splinting and applying compression wraps.	28
E. Exertional Heat-Related Illnesses	Watch a DVD segment "Responding to Heat-Related Illnesses."	5
F. Unit Summary	Review key unit points.	2

UNIT CONTENT

A Unit Introduction (1 minute)

- Conducting the physical assessment
- Types of bleeding and how to control bleeding
- Treating shock
- Splinting
- Applying compression wraps
- Using PRICE—protection, rest, ice, compression, and elevation—to minimize local tissue damage
- Responding to heat-related illnesses

B Physical Assessment (7 minutes)

Sport First Aid Quick Reference Card

Remember that the Sport First Aid Quick Reference Card is two-sided: One side illustrates the emergency action steps, and the other side illustrates the physical assessment. The side with the physical assessment provides a quick reminder of how to conduct a physical assessment. It includes steps you should follow to

- determine the history of the injury or illness,
- inspect the athlete for symptoms and signs of injury or illness, and
- use the sense of touch to feel for additional symptoms and signs of injury or illness.

As you watch the DVD segment, follow along on the Quick Reference Card.

On the DVD Segment, "Physical Assessment: History, Inspection, and Touch"

- The physical assessment: HIT
  - History
  - Inspection
  - Touch

- Overview of basic sport first aid techniques

C Controlling Bleeding and Protecting Against Blood-Borne Pathogens (17 minutes)

On the DVD Segment, "Controlling Bleeding"

- Preventing blood-borne pathogen transmission
- Causes, signs, and symptoms of profuse (arterial and venous) and slow, steady (capillary) bleeding
- Controlling arterial and venous bleeding
- Controlling slow, steady bleeding
- Playing it safe with bleeding injuries

Activity 5.1 Controlling Bleeding

Introduction

As you heard on the DVD segment, there are three main ways to control bleeding:

- Cover the wound with sterile gauze pads.
- Apply direct pressure.
- Apply elastic roller gauze or elastic bandage over the gauze pads.

In this activity, you'll practice these methods of controlling bleeding.

Resources

- The Controlling Bleeding Scenario (provided after the following instructions and activity outcome)
- Disposable gloves (one pair for each coach)
- Gauze pads (three for each coach)
- Elastic wrap or roller gauze (one for each coach)

Instructions

1. Work in pairs. One person will be the athlete, and one person will be the coach.
2. First review the Controlling Bleeding Scenario, and then follow the steps in the scenario.
3. When the coach has completed the scenario, reverse roles and repeat the entire scenario so that both partners have a chance to practice all skills.
4. You'll have 7 minutes to complete this activity, with each person in the coach's role for a little under 4 minutes.

Activity Outcome

When you're done, you should have completed the Controlling Bleeding Scenario two times—with each person having played the role of the coach.

▶ Controlling Bleeding Scenario -

The athlete (your partner) has a bleeding injury suffered while diving to save a volleyball. The athlete's wrist hit the volleyball standard, leaving a deep gash below the palm. You've completed the physical assessment and identified one injury requiring immediate attention: the bleeding wrist. After sending for medical assistance and putting a pair of disposable gloves on your hands, administer first aid for profuse bleeding.

1. Cover the wound with sterile gauze pads.
2. Apply firm, direct pressure over the wound with your hand. (The bleeding does not stop.)
3. Apply elastic roller gauze or elastic bandage over the gauze pads. Make sure it's not so tight that a finger can't be slipped under the bandage. (The bleeding stops.)
4. Leave the gauze in place, add more gauze if necessary, and cover with roller gauze or elastic wrap.
5. Monitor breathing and circulation until medical assistance arrives.

D Controlling Tissue Damage (Shock), Applying Splints, and Applying Compression Wraps (28 minutes)

On the DVD Segment, "Shock, Splints, and Compression Wraps"

- Shock: definition, its effects, causes, symptoms, signs, first aid steps
- Playing it safe when treating for shock
- Splinting: when, what, and how to splint (with demonstration)
- Playing it safe with splinting
- Local tissue damage: causes, symptoms, signs
- PRICE: definition and demonstration, including demonstration of compression wraps
- Types of ice applications (demonstration) and guidelines for applying each
- Contraindications to applying ice
- Playing it safe with applying heat

Activity 5.2 Positioning an Ill or Injured Athlete

Introduction

As you heard on the DVD segment, if the athlete is in shock, you may need to position the athlete properly. This also holds for other types of injuries and medical conditions.

- Proper positioning of an injured athlete depends on whether the athlete is injured or not, has a head or spine injury, is responsive or unresponsive, is breathing, or is in shock.
- In this activity, we'll decide as a class how to position an ill or injured athlete.

Resources

- The Positioning an Ill or Injured Athlete Scenarios on page 32
- The table, Positions for Ill or Injured Athletes, on page 33

Instructions

1. We'll work together as a class.

2. We'll have two volunteers who will play the role of ill or injured athletes.

3. We'll use the Positioning an Ill or Injured Athlete Scenarios and the table, Positions for Ill or Injured Athletes, on page 33 in the study guide to decide how to position each of our volunteer athletes.

4. We have about 8 minutes for this activity.

Activity Outcome

When we're done, we will have positioned two ill or injured athletes in the correct position for their conditions.

▶ Positioning an Ill or Injured Athlete Scenario I - - - - - - - - - - - - - - -

A football player is lying on the ground. You did not see the injury occur. He is responsive. You check the athlete's airway and breathing and find that the athlete is breathing normally.

You begin the physical assessment by asking the athlete what caused the injury. In a groggy voice, the athlete answers that he had run into a lineman head first. You ask the athlete if he heard a pop, crack, or other noise. The athlete tells you that he only heard his helmet as he hit the ground. The athlete doesn't have a clear idea of where he hurts, but he does tell you that his head snapped and his fingers are tingly. His head hurts, his ears are ringing, and he feels nauseated. He also says he's having trouble seeing, that everything's blurry.

1. In what position should you place the athlete? Why?

▶ Positioning an Ill or Injured Athlete Scenario II - - - - - - - - - - - - - -

A rowing crew team member slips on the dock and falls, grazing his leg on a sharp post that deeply lacerates his leg. The cut is bleeding rapidly, and the blood looks dark red. The athlete is lying flat on his back on the dock. You have put on goggles and gloves and have covered the wound with gauze pads. While you hold the pads down with firm, direct pressure, you examine the athlete and notice that he's breathing more slowly than usual, his pupils are dilated, and he's sweating. You ask him how he's feeling, and he says he feels weak and thirsty and would like a drink.

1. Is it necessary to reposition the athlete? Why?

2. Should you give the athlete something to drink? Why or why not?

Positions for Ill or Injured Athletes

CONDITION	POSITION	RATIONALE
Responsive athlete with suspected spinal injury	Manually stabilize the head so that the head, neck, and spine do not move and are kept in line (see figure 5.6).	Pain and loss of function usually accompany a spinal injury, but the absence of pain does not mean that the athlete has not been significantly injured. If you suspect an athlete could possibly have a spinal injury, assume they do.
Unresponsive, uninjured athlete who is breathing, but having difficulty with secretions or vomiting	Recovery Position	Protects airway by allowing fluid to drain easily from the mouth.
Unresponsive, injured athlete who is breathing, but having difficulty with secretions or vomiting OR who you must leave unattended to get help	Modified Recovery Position (HAINES)	Protects airway by allowing fluid to drain easily from the mouth. Using the HAINES position, there is less neck movement and less risk of spinal-cord damage.
Unresponsive athlete who is not breathing (or you are unsure)	Flat on the back for CPR	Occasional gasps are not normal and are not capable of supplying the athlete with enough oxygen to sustain life.
Responsive or unresponsive athlete with signs and symptoms of shock from severe bleeding	Flat on the back	It is best to leave the athlete lying flat. If athlete is having difficulty with secretions or vomiting, place in the recovery position. If spinal injury is suspected, use the HAINES position.

Activity 5.3 Splinting and Compression Wraps

Introduction

Now let's practice applying splints and compression wraps.

Resources

- The Splinting Scenario and Compression Wrap Scenario (see pages 34 to 35)
- Chapter 5 of *Sport First Aid*
- Rigid, padded splints for a broken arm (enough for half the class)
- Pillows, sweatshirts, or towels for the splinting activity (enough for half the class)
- Ties or elastic wrap to secure a splint (enough for half the class)
- Elastic wrap to secure a splint to the body and to use for a compression wrap (enough for half the class)

Instructions

1. Work in pairs. One person will be the athlete, and one person will be the coach. You'll complete two scenarios.

2. First review the Splinting Scenario, and then follow the steps in the scenario.

3. When the coach has completed the Splinting Scenario, reverse roles and repeat the scenario so that both partners have a chance to practice all skills.

4. Then review the Compression Wrap Scenario, and follow the steps in the scenario.

5. When the coach has completed the Compression Wrap Scenario, reverse roles and repeat the scenario so that both partners have a chance to practice all skills.

6. You'll have 15 minutes to do this activity. You should spend about 10 minutes splinting (5 minutes for each person) and 5 minutes applying the compression wrap (2 and a half minutes for each person).

Activity Outcome

When you're done, both of you should have practiced splinting a broken arm and applying a compression wrap to a sprained ankle.

▶ Splinting Scenario -

Your partner is a gymnast who has suffered a possible fractured forearm, just below the elbow. The injured arm is straight and held near the athlete's side. You have already completed a physical assessment. You find out that the arrival of EMS will be delayed for more than 20 minutes, so you apply a splint to the area.

1. Leave the arm in the position that you found it.

2. Place a pillow, sweatshirt, or towel between the arm and the body to help support the arm.

3. Immobilize the arm from the hand to above the elbow joint using a rigid, padded splint.

4. Secure the splint with ties or an elastic wrap. Place ties above and below the injury, but not directly over it. Apply light, even pressure with the wrap, so as not to press directly upon the injury.

5. Immobilize the entire arm, securing it to the body with an elastic wrap.

6. Check the radial pulse.

7. Compare your splint with the one shown in figure 5.9, page 75, of *Sport First Aid.*

8. Reverse roles and repeat the entire scenario so that both partners have a chance to practice all skills.

▶ *Compression Wrap Scenario-* -

Your partner is a softball player who twisted her ankle running to first base. You have already completed a physical assessment and have begun the PRICE sequence. You have protected the athlete from further movement, helped her to the bench where she can rest, removed her shoe, and applied an ice bag for 15 minutes. Now apply a compression wrap.

1. Start the wrap just above the toes.

2. Wrap upward (toward the heart), in an overlapping spiral, starting with even and somewhat snug pressure, then gradually wrapping looser once above the injury.

3. Periodically check the skin color, temperature, and sensation of the injured area to make sure that the wrap isn't compressing any nerves or arteries. Wraps that are too tight can reduce blood flow to the area and cause tissue damage.

4. Compare your compression wrap with the one shown in figure 5.18, page 80, of *Sport First Aid.*

5. Reverse roles and repeat the entire scenario so that both partners have a chance to practice all skills.

E Exertional Heat-Related Illnesses (5 minutes)

On the DVD Segment, "Responding to Heat-Related Illnesses"

- Heat cramps
- Heat exhaustion
- Heatstroke

F Unit Summary (2 minutes)

- After you've checked the ABCs of airway, breathing, and circulation and have established that the athlete is breathing, you should conduct the physical assessment to determine the nature, site, and severity of an injury or illness.

- Remember the acronym HIT—which stands for history, inspection, and touch. This will help you complete a thorough physical assessment.
- After completing the physical assessment, you should attend to these issues, in this order of priority:

    1. Control profuse external bleeding.
    2. Minimize shock.
    3. Splint unstable injuries.
    4. Use the PRICE method to minimize local tissue damage.

- PRICE stands for protection, rest, ice, compression, and elevation.
- When an athlete suffers a heat-related illness, prompt action is key. If the athlete shows signs of possible heatstroke, send for emergency medical assistance and immediately cool the athlete in a wading pool or tub filled with ice water.

Unit 5 Activity Outcomes

▶ *Emergency Action Steps—Activity 5.2 Outcome* - - - - - - - - - - - - -

POSITIONING FOR ILL OR INJURED ATHLETE SCENARIO 1

1. In what position should you place the athlete? Why?

Because he has a potential head or spine injury, this athlete's head and neck should be immobilized with the athlete lying face up and flat on the ground.

POSITIONING FOR ILL OR INJURED ATHLETE SCENARIO 2

1. Is it necessary to reposition the athlete? Why?

This athlete should remain flat on his back, as he seems to be going into shock from severe bleeding. (Do not raise his legs; this was once advocated, but current evidence does not support this practice.) However, if you think he may be about to vomit, you may want to move him into the recovery position. If you reposition the athlete, you'll need to maintain direct pressure on the wound to continue controlling the bleeding.

2. Should you give the athlete something to drink? Why or why not?

This athlete should not be given anything to drink. You should not give fluids to an athlete who is suffering from shock. Doing so can cause vomiting or choking.

Moving Injured or Sick Athletes

(10 minutes)

PURPOSE: To help you learn how to determine whether and how an injured or sick athlete should be moved.

LEARNING OBJECTIVES

In this unit, you will learn

- how to determine whether an athlete should be moved;
- how to decide who should move an athlete and how the athlete should be moved; and
- how to do the four- or five-person rescue, the one-person drag, the one-person walking assist, the two-person walking assist, the four-handed carrying assist, and the two-handed carrying assist.

Unit Overview

Topic	Activities	Time (minutes)
A. Unit Introduction	Hear about the unit's purpose, objectives, and agenda.	1
B. Moving an Athlete	Watch a DVD segment, "Moving Injured or Sick Athletes." Practice techniques for moving athletes.	8
C. Unit Summary	Review key unit points.	1

UNIT CONTENT

A Unit Introduction (I minute)

- Whether to move an athlete
- Playing it safe when moving athletes
- Techniques for moving critically injured and noncritically injured athletes

B Moving an Athlete (8 minutes)

On the DVD Segment, "Moving Injured or Sick Athletes"

- To move or not to move an athlete
- Playing it safe when moving critically injured, unresponsive athletes
- Techniques for moving critically injured athletes: four- or five-person rescue and one-person drag
- Playing it safe when moving noncritically injured athletes
- Techniques for moving noncritically injured athletes: one-person walking assist, two-person walking assist, four-handed carrying assist, and two-handed carrying assist
- Playing it safe to protect yourself

Activity 6.1 Moving an Athlete

Introduction

To move an athlete safely, you need to know how to correctly perform each technique. In this activity, you'll get to practice three techniques for moving athletes.

Resources

- The Two-Person Walking Assist Scenario, and Two-Handed Carrying Assist Scenario (provided after the following instructions and activity outcome)
- Pages 87 and 88 in the *Sport First Aid* book, which show photos of each technique

Instructions

1. Work in groups of three to four.
2. First review the Two-Person Walking Assist Scenario and Two-Handed Carrying Assist Scenario, and then follow the steps in each scenario.

3. All members of your group should practice the techniques.
4. Take 4 to 5 minutes to complete this activity.

Activity Outcome

When you're done, you should have practiced as many of the techniques as possible: the two-person walking assist and the two-handed carrying assist.

▶ Two-Person Walking Assist Scenario -

An athlete is sitting down on the field, but otherwise shows no sign of injury. He complains of being slightly dazed from contact with an opposing player. The technique you should use to move the athlete to the sideline is the **TWO-PERSON WALKING ASSIST.**

1. Kneel on one knee on opposite sides of the athlete.
2. Place the athlete's arms around you (and your partner) and instruct the athlete to hold onto your shoulders.
3. Hold the athlete around the waist.
4. On the count of three, bring the athlete to a standing position.
5. Slowly walk to the sidelines, supporting the athlete with your arms and shoulders.

▶ Two-Handed Carrying Assist Scenario - - - - - - - - - - - - - - - - - - -

An athlete has a badly strained calf muscle and is unable to walk or help support her weight. The technique you should use to move the athlete is the **TWO-HANDED CARRYING ASSIST,** which requires two people.

1. Stand behind the injured athlete, facing your partner.
2. Grasp each other's forearms nearest the athlete.
3. Instruct the athlete to sit on your and your partner's arms and to put his or her arms around your shoulders.
4. Support the athlete's back with your free arms.
5. Slowly lift the athlete by straightening your legs.

C Unit Summary (1 minute)

- Before moving an athlete, determine if it is necessary and safe to do so.

- If an athlete must be moved, carefully decide which method should be used to move the athlete.

- For critically injured athletes, consider the four- or five-person rescue, or the one-person drag.

- For noncritically injured athletes, consider the one-person walking assist, two-person walking assist, four-handed carrying assist, and two-handed carrying assist.

Closed Head and Spine Injuries

(20 minutes)

PURPOSE: To help you learn how to identify and provide first aid care for closed head and spine injuries.

LEARNING OBJECTIVES

In this unit, you will learn

- how to recognize the signs and symptoms of head and spine injuries,
- what first aid care to provide for responsive and unresponsive athletes with head or spine injuries, and
- what head and spine injury prevention strategies you can incorporate into your sport first aid game plan.

Unit Overview

Topic	Activities	Time (minutes)
A. Unit Introduction	Hear about the unit's purpose, objectives, and agenda.	1
B. First Aid for Closed Head and Spine Injuries	Watch a DVD segment, "Responding to Closed Head and Spine Injuries." Practice identifying head and spine injuries and determining the first aid steps needed.	18
C. Unit Summary	Review key unit points.	1

UNIT CONTENT

A Unit Introduction (1 minute)

- Identifying closed head and spine injuries
- Determining what first aid steps to take
- Steps you can take to help prevent head and spine injuries

B First Aid for Closed Head and Spine Injuries (18 minutes)

On the DVD Segment, "Responding to Closed Head and Spine Injuries"

- Percentages of reported head, neck, and spine injuries by sport
- Closed head injuries: concussion, contusion, hemorrhage and hematoma, and fracture
- Spine injuries: sprains, contusions, strains, and fractures

Part III of Sport First Aid

- Read the introduction to part III, pages 91 to 92, in *Sport First Aid.*
- Over 110 different conditions are covered.
- The chapters are ordered from life-threatening conditions to serious then minor problems.
- For each condition, detailed information is given, including symptoms, signs, and first aid steps.

Activity 7.1 Closed Head and Spine Injuries

Introduction

The key with closed head and spine injuries is to recognize that an athlete may have such an injury. Once you have determined that an athlete may have a closed head or spine injury, the first aid care you provide will be quite similar for either type.

Resources

- The Closed Head and Spine Injury Scenarios (provided after the following instructions and activity outcome)
- Chapter 8 of *Sport First Aid,* which begins on page 101

Instructions

1. Work in teams of two to four.
2. Read the Closed Head and Spine Injury Scenarios, and answer the questions posed.
3. This is a team competition; teams will be awarded points for correct answers.
4. Take 8 minutes to complete your work.

Activity Outcome

When you're done, you should have identified the possible injury in each scenario and the first aid steps you would take to care for the injury.

▶ *Closed Head and Spine Injury Scenario 1* - - - - - - - - - - - - - - - - -

One of your athletes is unresponsive and lying on the basketball court. She has clear fluid draining from her nose and ears, and her pupils do not constrict to light.

1. What injury do you believe this athlete has? Use chapter 8 of *Sport First Aid,* pages 103 to 113, to help make your decision.

2. What first aid steps would you take to care for this injury? Record the steps in the space below.

▶ *Closed Head and Spine Injury Scenario 2* - - - - - - - - - - - - - - - - - -

One of your wrestlers walks from the mat and tells you that his lower back hurts. You ask a few questions and find that his pain is near his spine. Upon further examination, you find that his toes are numb.

1. What injury do you believe this athlete has? Use chapter 8 of *Sport First Aid,* pages 103 to 113, to help make your decision.

2. What first aid steps would you take to care for this injury? Record the steps in the space below.

C Unit Summary (1 minute)

- There is no such thing as a minor brain or spine injury. Even minor concussions injure the brain and should not be taken lightly.
- Regardless of the head or spine injury, the first aid response is very similar.
- If an athlete is responsive but you suspect a concussion, remove the athlete from play. Assign someone to monitor the athlete for signs and symptoms of a moderate or severe head injury. If such signs or symptoms occur, send for emergency medical assistance. For a suspected mild concussion, notify the parents. Ask them to monitor the athlete, and give them a checklist of head injury signs and symptoms. Instruct them to take the athlete to a physician.
- If you suspect a head or spine injury in a football player, do not attempt to remove the athlete's helmet.

Unit 7 Activity Outcomes

CLOSED HEAD AND SPINE INJURY SCENARIO 1

- *Injury:* Any head or spine injury is possible, but the athlete most likely is unresponsive with a closed head injury.
- *First aid steps:*
  1. Send for emergency medical assistance. **2 PT**
  2. Immobilize the athlete's head and spine. **2 PTS**
  3. Monitor breathing and circulation and provide CPR if needed. **2 PTS**
  4. Control profuse bleeding. **2 PTS**
  5. Treat for shock as needed. **2 PTS**
  6. Stabilize any other fractures, dislocations, sprains, or strains. **2 PTS**

TOTAL POINTS POSSIBLE: 12

CLOSED HEAD AND SPINE INJURY SCENARIO 2

- *Injury:* Any head or spine injury is possible, but the athlete most likely has a spine injury.
- *First aid steps:*
  1. Send for emergency medical assistance. **2 PTS**
  2. Immobilize the athlete's head and spine. **2 PTS**
  3. Monitor breathing and circulation and provide CPR if needed. **2 PTS**
  4. Control profuse bleeding. **2 PTS**
  5. Treat for shock as needed. **2 PTS**
  6. Stabilize any other fractures, dislocations, sprains, or strains. **2 PTS**

TOTAL POINTS POSSIBLE: 24

Each first aid step is worth 2 points, for a total of 24 points for both injuries.

Musculoskeletal Injuries

(35 minutes)

PURPOSE: To help you learn how to identify and provide first aid care for the most common sprains, strains, fractures, and dislocations.

LEARNING OBJECTIVES

In this unit, you will learn

- how to recognize common musculoskeletal injuries and
- how to provide first aid care for sprains, strains, fractures, and dislocations.

Unit Overview

Topic	Activities	Time (minutes)
A. Unit Introduction	Hear about the unit's purpose, objectives, and agenda.	1
B. Recognizing and Caring for Common Musculoskeletal Injuries	Watch a DVD segment, "Musculoskeletal Injuries." Practice identifying common musculoskeletal injuries and taking the first aid steps needed.	32
C. Unit Summary	Review key unit points.	2

UNIT CONTENT

A Unit Introduction (1 minute)

- The main types of musculoskeletal injuries
- Identifying musculoskeletal injuries to various body parts
- Determining what first aid steps to take

B Recognizing and Caring for Common Musculoskeletal Injuries (32 minutes)

On the DVD Segment, "Musculoskeletal Injuries"

- Commonly occurring musculoskeletal injuries
- The main types of musculoskeletal injuries
- General first aid steps to take with these injuries

Activity 8.1 Musculoskeletal Injuries

Introduction

Musculoskeletal injuries are the most frequent first aid problem you will face. In this activity, you'll practice identifying injuries, and you'll write a list of first aid steps you would take for each injury.

Resources

- The Musculoskeletal Injury Scenarios (provided after the following instructions and activity outcome)
- Chapters 12 and 13 of *Sport First Aid.* Chapter 12 begins on page 149.

Instructions

1. Work in teams of two to four.
2. Read the Musculoskeletal Injury Scenarios, and answer the questions posed.
3. This is another team competition. Points will be awarded for correct answers: 2 points for correctly identifying the injury, 1 point for correctly identifying the severity or Grade (if there is one), and 3 points for including all first aid steps. Your team will receive 0 points for the first aid section unless *all* steps are included. There are 34 possible points.
4. You'll have 24 minutes to complete this activity.

Activity Outcome

When you're done, you should have identified the injury in each scenario and the first aid steps you would take to care for each injury. Points will be awarded for correct injury identification and first aid steps.

▶ *Musculoskeletal Injury Scenario 1* -

One of your swimmers comes to you after practice complaining of a sore shoulder. You ask a few questions and find that the swimmer's shoulder hurts when he lifts his arm overhead. In your physical assessment, you examine his shoulder with your fingers and find that he has mild tenderness over the front of his shoulder. He has been swimming with the sore shoulder for a week and has just now mentioned the problem. You had not noticed any change in his swimming performance.

1. What injury do you believe this athlete has? Use chapter 12 of *Sport First Aid,* pages 149 to 162, to help make your decision.

2. Is this injury a Grade I, II, or III injury?

3. What first aid steps would you take to care for this injury? Record the steps in the space below.

▶ *Musculoskeletal Injury Scenario 2* -

Your softball pitcher is hit hard in the upper trunk by the ball. She crumples in pain. Her breathing is normal, but she has pain when she breathes deeply or laughs. The athlete experiences pain when you gently compress the rib cage.

1. What injury do you believe this athlete has? Use chapter 12 of *Sport First Aid,* pages 162 to 163, to help make your decision.

2. What first aid steps would you take to care for this injury? Record the steps in the space below.

▶ *Musculoskeletal Injury Scenario 3* -

Your star wrestler seems to have hurt his middle finger while catching himself during a fall. The wrestler says he felt a pop and that his finger feels "loose." He is unable to fully bend his finger. You can see that the finger is swollen and deformed, and when you touch the joint, the wrestler grimaces in pain.

1. What injury do you believe this athlete has? Use chapter 12 of *Sport First Aid,* pages 177 to 184, to help make your decision.

2. What first aid steps would you take to care for this injury? Record the steps in the space below.

▶ *Musculoskeletal Injury Scenario 4* -

When the kicker on your football team pulls up short after a punt, you know something is wrong. You and your assistant jog out on the field and help the player walk to the sidelines. The athlete has moderate pain when trying to extend his thigh backward or bend his knee. The back of his thigh is tender, and you can feel a slight indentation there.

1. What injury do you believe this athlete has? Use chapter 13 of *Sport First Aid,* pages 192 to 203, to help make your decision.

2. Is this injury a Grade I, II, or III injury?

3. What first aid steps would you take to care for this injury? Record the steps in the space below.

▶ *Musculoskeletal Injury Scenario 5* -

The guard on your girls' basketball team lost her footing and twisted her knee as she scrambled to reposition for a play. You quickly substituted another player so that she could come off the court. The athlete says she didn't hear or feel a pop, but she has mild pain when she tries to straighten her knee. There is no swelling.

1. What injury do you believe this athlete has? Use chapter 13 of *Sport First Aid,* pages 203 to 211, to help make your decision.

2. Is this injury a Grade I, II, or III injury?

3. What first aid steps would you take to care for this injury? Record the steps in the space below.

▶ *Musculoskeletal Injury Scenario 6* -

One of your volleyball players landed wrong coming down from a spike. Her foot rolled inward, and she is writhing in pain. Her breathing and circulation are normal, but her ankle is swelling rapidly and she cannot walk on it. Her ankle has no obvious deformity, and she experiences no pain when you squeeze above or below the injury. She has no tingling or numbness, and her toes and toenails are normal in color. Her point tenderness seems isolated to just below the ankle bones, but the pain there is severe.

1. What injury do you believe this athlete has? Use chapter 13 of *Sport First Aid,* pages 211 to 225, to help make your decision.

2. Is this injury a Grade I, II, or III injury?

3. What first aid steps would you take to care for this injury? Record the steps in the space below.

C Unit Summary (2 minutes)

- You will likely deal with musculoskeletal injuries more than any other type of injury.

- Chapters 12 and 13 of *Sport First Aid* can be used for guidance in identifying and providing first aid care for musculoskeletal injuries.

- Once the injury is identified, the first aid steps are similar regardless of the type and severity of injury:

  - For Grade I sprains and strains, rest the athlete from painful activities, apply ice, and refer the athlete to a physician if symptoms and signs worsen or do not subside within a few days.

  - For Grade II and III sprains and strains, rest the athlete from all activities, prevent the athlete from using the injured part (if a Grade III sprain or strain, be sure to immobilize the injured part with a splint and possibly a sling), monitor and treat for shock if needed and send for emergency medical assistance if it occurs, and apply ice and send to a physician if shock does not occur.

  - For fractures, immobilize the injured part, apply ice, and send for emergency medical assistance if bones are grossly displaced or protruding.

Unit 8 Activity Outcomes

MUSCULOSKELETAL INJURY SCENARIO I

- *Injury:* Rotator cuff strain. **2 PTS**
- *Severity:* Grade I. **I PT**
- *First aid steps:* 1. Rest from painful activities; 2. Apply ice; 3. Refer to a physician if symptoms and signs worsen or do not subside within a few days. **3 PTS**

MUSCULOSKELETAL INJURY SCENARIO 2

- *Injury:* Rib fracture. **2 PTS**
- *First aid steps:* 1. Rest from all activities; 2. If the athlete has breathing difficulties, an open chest wound, or a backward displaced (toward internal organs) rib, or the athlete is suffering from shock, call for emergency medical assistance; 3. If none of the above apply, send the athlete to a physician. **3 PTS**

MUSCULOSKELETAL INJURY SCENARIO 3

- *Injury:* Finger dislocation. **2 PTS**
- *First aid steps:* 1. Send for emergency medical assistance if the athlete is suffering from shock or there are signs of nerve damage or disrupted circulation; 2. If none of the above, immobilize the hand and finger in the position in which you found them; 3. Monitor and treat for shock as needed; 4. Apply ice; 5. Send to a physician. **3 PTS**

MUSCULOSKELETAL INJURY SCENARIO 4

- *Injury:* Hamstring strain. **2 PTS**
- *Severity:* Grade II—the key word is *moderate.* **I PT**
- *First aid steps:* 1. Rest from all activities; 2. Monitor and treat for shock as needed and send for emergency medical assistance if it occurs; 3. Send for emergency medical assistance if the muscle is completely torn (rolled up); 4. Prevent the athlete from walking on the injured leg; 5. Apply ice to the injury and send the athlete to a physician (if emergency medical assistance is not sent for). **3 PTS**

MUSCULOSKELETAL INJURY SCENARIO 5

- *Injury:* Knee sprain. **2 PTS**
- *Severity:* Grade I. **1 PT**
- *First aid steps:* 1. Rest the athlete from painful activities; 2. Apply ice; 3. Refer the athlete to a physician if symptoms and signs worsen or do not subside within a few days. **3 PTS**

MUSCULOSKELETAL INJURY SCENARIO 6

- *Injury:* Ankle sprain. **2 PTS**
- *Severity:* Grade II or III—either answer is acceptable for this scenario. **1 PT**
- *First aid steps:* 1. Rest the athlete from all activities that require use of the leg; 2. Prevent the athlete from walking on the injured leg; 3. Monitor and treat for shock as needed and send for emergency medical assistance if it occurs; 4. Send for emergency medical assistance if any of the following are present: (a) signs of fracture—obvious deformity or pain at the site of the injury when tibia and fibula are gently squeezed above or below the injury, or pain along the midline of the lower third of the tibia or fibula; (b) symptoms and signs of nerve compression (tingling and numbness); (c) symptoms and signs of disrupted blood supply (bluish toes and toenails); 5. Apply ice to the injury and send the athlete to a physician (if emergency medical assistance is not sent for). **3 PTS**

TOTAL POINTS POSSIBLE: 34

Sport First Aid Wrap-Up

(20 minutes)

PURPOSE: To help you review what has been learned in the class and understand the process and procedures for completing the rest of the Sport First Aid course.

LEARNING OBJECTIVES

In this unit, you will learn

- answers to any of your remaining questions and
- the process and procedures for completing the rest of the Sport First Aid course.

Unit Overview

Topic	Activities	Time (minutes)
A. Unit Introduction	Hear about the unit's purpose, objectives, and agenda.	1
B. Sport First Aid Classroom Course Summary	Review the main topics covered in the course. Ask any remaining questions about first aid steps.	4
C. Sport First Aid Classroom Course Evaluation	Complete Activity 9.1 Course Evaluation.	5
D. Completing the Sport First Aid Self-Study Units and Test	Participate in Activity 9.2 Self-Study Procedures. Then participate in Activity 9.3 Testing Procedures.	8
E. Goodbye and Thanks	Final questions and goodbyes.	2

UNIT CONTENT

A Unit Introduction (1 minute)

- Ask any remaining questions
- Fill out a course evaluation
- Learn the procedures for completing the self-study portion and the course test

B Sport First Aid Classroom Course Summary (4 minutes)

Today we have discussed

- your role on the athletic health care team,
- types of injuries and illnesses and how they occur,
- conducting the emergency action steps and providing life support,
- conducting the physical assessment and providing immediate first aid,
- moving injured or sick athletes,
- closed head and spine injuries, and
- musculoskeletal injuries.

C Sport First Aid Classroom Course Evaluation (5 minutes)

Activity 9.1 Course Evaluation

Introduction

We are interested in knowing your reactions to this course, so we'd like you to complete a course evaluation. Your evaluation will be used to make improvements in future courses.

Resources

- Sport First Aid Classroom Test Package, including
  - an ASEP Bronze Level Evaluation Form to evaluate the course,
  - a Sport First Aid Classroom Test,
  - an ASEP Test Answer Form A to record test answers,
  - the Sport First Aid Test Instructions,

- a preaddressed ASEP mailing envelope for you to mail the completed ASEP Test Answer Form A,
- a cardboard insert to ensure that the test form is not damaged in the mail.

Instructions

1. Review the marking instructions for completing the ASEP Bronze Level Evaluation Form.
2. At the top of the evaluation, enter the instructor's identification number, the instructor's last name, and today's date, which is the last date of the course.
3. Find the course code on the last page of the Sport First Aid Classroom Test, and enter it as the course code on the evaluation. The course code should be either BB10, BB11, or BB12.
4. Complete the rest of the evaluation.
5. Hand in your completed evaluation to the instructor.

Activity Outcome

When you're done, you should have completed and handed in the evaluation.

D Completing the Sport First Aid Self-Study and Test (8 minutes)

Activity 9.2 Self-Study Procedures

Introduction

Over the next several weeks, you need to complete the self-study portion of the course and the Sport First Aid Test.

- Complete these activities by _____.
- If you do not successfully pass your Sport First Aid Test within six months of the last date of your course, you will have to take the entire course over again and pay all of the course fees again.

Table of Contents for the Self-Study

- An introductory unit (unit 1)
- A wrap-up unit that discusses taking the course test (unit 17)
- 15 other units, one unit for each chapter in the text, *Sport First Aid.*

Example: Unit 2, Your Role on the Athletic Health Care Team

- Lists the learning objectives for the unit.
- Indicates which chapter to read in *Sport First Aid*.
- Includes activities and activity solutions to help you learn and apply the concepts and skills covered in the chapter.

Activity 9.3 Testing Procedures

Introduction

The last thing you'll do to complete the course is to complete the course test.

Resources

To complete the test, you'll need

- the Sport First Aid Test Instructions,
- the Sport First Aid Classroom Test,
- the ASEP Test Answer Form A,
- a pencil or black or blue ballpoint pen, and
- the text, *Sport First Aid*.

Test Procedures

- Three things to do:
    1. Decide whether you'll complete the test paper-pencil or online.
    2. Complete the test.
    3. Get your test scored.
- The course test can be completed paper-pencil, using the Sport First Aid Classroom Test and ASEP Test Answer Form A, or it can be completed online using the Sport First Aid Online Test.
- The course test is open book. You can refer to *Sport First Aid* and any other course materials while you complete the test. However, you should complete the test individually—*it is not a team activity*.
- If you do not pass the test the first time, you can take it again. The procedures for retests are described in the test instructions.

Important Points About the Test

- Both the classroom and online tests test the same content and include 50 multiple-choice and 25 true/false questions. Each test includes questions for each chapter in the text, *Sport First Aid*.

- The passing score for the test—whether paper-pencil or online—is 80 percent.
- There are three forms (or versions) of the classroom test. Which form you get is determined by chance.
- The questions for the online test are randomly generated from a pool of 225 questions—the same questions used to create the three forms of the classroom test. Consequently, there are virtually thousands of forms (or versions) of the online test. Which form you get is determined by chance.
- No two forms of the test—whether classroom or online—include all of the same questions. **IF YOU TAKE THE TEST ONLINE, THE ONLINE TEST WILL NOT INCLUDE THE SAME QUESTIONS THAT ARE ON THE PAPER-PENCIL TEST INCLUDED IN YOUR SPORT FIRST AID CLASSROOM TEST PACKAGE.**
- The online test is scored immediately so that you get your score within seconds of completing the test. The paper-pencil test must be sent into ASEP for scoring, and it takes about three weeks to get your score.
- Once you begin taking the test online, you can't change your mind and take the paper-pencil test, because the code that you enter online will "deactivate" the code on your scan form.
- If you need to complete a retest, you must complete the retest in the same way—paper-pencil or online—you completed the original test. If you took the original test paper-pencil, you must take the retest paper-pencil. And if you took the original test online, you must take the retest online.
- The test form you use for the retest will have different questions than the form you used the first time.
- The retest fee for the paper-pencil test is $20. The retest fee for the online test is $10.

Sport First Aid Test Instructions

- Instructions include specific steps for completing the test online—step 2 in the instructions—and for completing the test paper-pencil—step 3 in the instructions.
- If you take the paper-pencil test, instructions for mailing your test to ASEP also are included in the test instructions.
- Information to enter:
  - Your key code. The key code is the 10-digit number printed on the back page of these instructions.
  - The instructor's identification number.
  - The instructor's last name.

- The organization code.
- The last date of course.
- Current CPR certification: This information is required for ASEP's Bronze Level Certification.
- For the paper-pencil test **ONLY,** you'll need to enter the course code. This is the same code you entered on the course evaluation. It is on the back page of the Sport First Aid Classroom Test, is four characters long, and begins with BB followed by two numbers.

Final Points About the Test

- Please do not throw away any of the pieces of your test package (other than the plastic shrink-wrap).
- Make sure you keep the cardboard too.
- Put this package in a safe place until you have read *Sport First Aid,* completed the self-study activities, and are ready to take the test.
- Should you lose your scan form or test instructions (containing your test key code), you will be charged a $10 replacement fee.

Instructor Contact Information

- Instructor's phone number: _____
- Instructor's e-mail address: _____
- Instructor's best days and times: _____

E Goodbye and Thanks (2 minutes)

- Questions?
- Goodbyes.

SPORT FIRST AID SELF-STUDY UNITS

Introduction to the Sport First Aid Self-Study Process

LEARNING OBJECTIVES

In this unit, you will learn

- the purpose,
- process, and
- benefits of completing the Sport First Aid self-study units.

WHAT TO READ

Read the following sections, which describe the purpose and objectives of the Sport First Aid self-study units and provide tips for getting the most out of the self-study process.

Purpose of the Self-Study Units

In the self-study portion of the course, you'll learn sport first aid material that was not presented in the classroom sessions. You'll need to know this material to pass the Sport First Aid Classroom Test. In the classroom portion of the course, you learned sport first aid techniques that were best presented in person, shown on the DVD, or practiced by you in the classroom. But that's only part of what you need to know to be a prepared first responder. Now you need to get into the *Sport First Aid* text and learn other details about providing first aid care to athletes.

This part of the study guide will serve as an invaluable learning tool after you have read the *Sport First Aid* text. In this self-study portion of the course, you'll be able to gauge your understanding of the material, brush up on weak areas, and prepare for the Sport First Aid Classroom Test.

Objectives of the Self-Study Units

The objectives of the Sport First Aid self-study units are to

- encourage you to read *Sport First Aid,*
- provide activities that will help you test your understanding of the material,
- challenge you to refer back to the book to refresh your memory if your answers are not correct,
- help you apply the general concepts you learn to a wide variety of injuries and illnesses, and
- develop your ability to use *Sport First Aid* as a resource when delivering first aid care to your athletes.

Getting the Most Out of the Sport First Aid Self-Study Process

How can you get the most out of the self-study process?

1. Read the related *Sport First Aid* chapter before beginning each self-study unit.
2. As you read *Sport First Aid,* write notes in the book, flag pages that include important points, and etch in your mind where in the book you can find each type of injury.
3. Do one unit at a time—first reading the chapter in the book and then completing the unit—and complete the units in order. The units are ordered in the same way as the topics in the book. This will help you learn where to find information in the book.
4. Try to complete each activity without looking in *Sport First Aid* or at the Unit Solutions, which are found at the end of each unit. This will give you the most accurate assessment of your level of understanding.
5. Don't fret if you don't get all the answers correct. No one besides you will see your work for this self-study portion of the course. Learn from your errors and build on your successes. Use the self-study units as a learning tool to help you prepare for the Sport First Aid Classroom Test.

SPORT FIRST AID SELF-STUDY RESOURCES

You'll need two resources to complete the Sport First Aid self-study process:

- *Sport First Aid, Fourth Edition*

- *Sport First Aid Classroom Study Guide* (the book you are currently reading)

Sport First Aid, Fourth Edition

You'll want to eventually read *Sport First Aid* in its entirety. We recommend that you read each chapter before completing its related self-study unit. Everything you need to know to pass the Sport First Aid Classroom Test is in that book. Remember that the Sport First Aid Classroom Test is an open-book test. You'll want to be very familiar with *Sport First Aid* before taking the test.

Sport First Aid Classroom Study Guide

Completing self-study units 2 to 17 in this study guide will help you pass the Sport First Aid Classroom Test. Complete the units in order, and check your answers against the solutions given at the end of each unit. If you find that you did not answer correctly, go back to *Sport First Aid* to refresh your memory and to gain a better understanding of the subject matter. In unit 17, you'll learn the process and procedures for taking the Sport First Aid Classroom Test.

Your Role on the Athletic Health Care Team

LEARNING OBJECTIVES

In this unit, you will learn

- what the athletic health care team is and who is part of it;
- what your role is on the athletic health care team;
- what first aid knowledge parents expect you to have;
- what types of physicians you might work with and what your role is in working with them;
- what emergency medical personnel, athletic trainers, and physical therapists do and what your role is in working with them; and
- why treatment and rehabilitation are important parts of first aid follow-up.

WHAT TO READ

Read chapter 1, "Your Role on the Athletic Health Care Team," in *Sport First Aid.*

ACTIVITY 2.1

First Aid Responsibilities of Athletic Health Care Team Members

Match the athletic health care team members with their primary sport first aid responsibilities. Write the letter of each responsibility on the blank line next to the team member who performs it.

Athletic health care team members	Primary sport first aid responsibilities
_____ 1. Athletes	a. Respond to emergency medical problems, immobilize serious injuries, and provide swift and safe transportation to emergency medical facilities.
_____ 2. Parents	b. Rehabilitate individuals suffering from disease or injury.
_____ 3. Coaches	c. Diagnose vision problems and eye disease.
_____ 4. Emergency medical technicians and paramedics	d. Ensure their child participates in preseason physicals, fitness screenings, and conditioning.
_____ 5. Physicians	e. Oversee the inspection, cleaning and maintenance, and storage of equipment; oversee equipment fitting.
_____ 6. Certified athletic trainers	f. Diagnose athletic injuries and illnesses. Prescribe illness and injury treatment and rehabilitation.
_____ 7. Physical therapists	g. Perform fitness assessments and develop and supervise specialized conditioning programs for athletes.
_____ 8. Dentists or oral surgeons	h. Report their own injuries and illnesses.
_____ 9. Optometrists	i. Evaluate and treat conditions and injuries of the mouth, teeth, and jaw.
_____ 10. Strength and conditioning coaches	j. Prevent, evaluate, treat, and rehabilitate athletic injuries.
_____ 11. Equipment managers	k. Act as first responder in providing first aid care if no medical personnel are present when an injury or illness occurs.

ACTIVITY 2.1

First Aid Responsibilities of Athletic Health Care Team Members

Athletic health care team members	Primary sport first aid responsibilities
__h__ 1. Athletes	h. Report their own injuries and illnesses.
__d__ 2. Parents	d. Ensure their child participates in preseason physicals, fitness screenings, and conditioning.
__k__ 3. Coaches	k. Act as first responder in providing first aid care if no medical personnel are present when an injury or illness occurs.
__a__ 4. Emergency medical technicians and paramedics	a. Respond to emergency medical problems, immobilize serious injuries, and provide swift and safe transportation to emergency medical facilities.
__f__ 5. Physicians	f. Diagnose athletic injuries and illnesses. Prescribe illness and injury treatment and rehabilitation.
__j__ 6. Certified athletic trainers	j. Prevent, evaluate, treat, and rehabilitate athletic injuries.
__b__ 7. Physical therapists	b. Rehabilitate individuals suffering from disease or injury.
__i__ 8. Dentists or oral surgeons	i. Evaluate and treat conditions and injuries of the mouth, teeth, and jaw.
__c__ 9. Optometrists	c. Diagnose vision problems and eye disease.
__g__ 10. Strength and conditioning coaches	g. Perform fitness assessments and develop and supervise specialized conditioning programs for athletes.
__e__ 11. Equipment managers	e. Oversee the inspection, cleaning and maintenance, and storage of equipment; oversee equipment fitting.

Sport First Aid Game Plan

LEARNING OBJECTIVES

In this unit, you will learn

- how to keep yourself educated about sport first aid;
- what health records you should keep for each athlete;
- how to develop and initiate a weather emergency plan;
- what to look for when checking facilities for hazards and equipment for proper fit and usage;
- what to include in a first aid kit;
- why you should incorporate preseason physicals, fitness screenings, and conditioning programs into your game plan; and
- how to develop a medical emergency plan.

WHAT TO READ

Read chapter 2, "Sport First Aid Game Plan," in *Sport First Aid*.

ACTIVITY 3.1

Health History Form and Emergency Information Card

To handle injuries effectively, you have to plan for them. Before the start of the season, you should collect a consent form, health history form, and emergency information card from each player.

- You can find a sample consent form on page 15 in *Sport First Aid.* Your school district may have a standard consent form for you to use.
- Health history forms will tell you whether any of your athletes have health problems that could affect their sports participation.
- In the event of an emergency, you must be able to contact the athlete's parents or guardian and physician. An emergency information card provides their names and numbers and also contains information on preexisting medical problems that may influence the treatment of an athlete. You should have all athletes' parents complete this card before the season.

1. Fill out the health history form on page 71 with information about yourself (to become familiar with the form).
2. Fill out the emergency medical card on page 72 with information about yourself (to become familiar with the card). Think about whether there are any changes you need to make to this card to match your coaching situation.

ACTIVITY 3.2

Weather Emergency Plan

Note: This is an optional activity if you do not have a current coaching position.

In this activity, you will develop a weather emergency plan for your current coaching position. Write your plans on the Weather Emergency Plan on page 73. You can then copy this plan and distribute it to those who need it.

Health History Form

Athletic Medical Examination for _____
(sport)

Name _____ Age _____ Birth date _____

Address _____ Phone _____
      (street)   (city)   (zip)

Instructions

All questions must be answered. Failure to disclose pertinent medical information may invalidate your insurance coverage and may cancel your eligibility to participate in interscholastic athletics. Any further health problems must be discussed with the physician at the time of this examination.

Medical History

Have you ever had any of the following? If "yes," give details to the examining doctor.

	No	Yes	Details (if answered yes)
1. Head injury or concussion	___	___	_____
2. Bone or joint disorders, fractures, dislocations, trick joints, arthritis, or back pain	___	___	_____
3. Eye or ear problems (disease or surgery)	___	___	_____
4. Heat illness	___	___	_____
5. Dizzy spells, fainting, or convulsions	___	___	_____
6. Tuberculosis, asthma, or bronchitis	___	___	_____
7. Heart trouble or rheumatic fever	___	___	_____
8. High or low blood pressure	___	___	_____
9. Anemia, leukemia, or bleeding disorder	___	___	_____
10. Diabetes, hepatitis, or jaundice	___	___	_____
11. Ulcers, other stomach trouble, or colitis	___	___	_____
12. Kidney or bladder problems	___	___	_____
13. Hernia (rupture)	___	___	_____
14. Mental illness or nervous breakdown	___	___	_____
15. Addiction to drugs or alcohol	___	___	_____
16. Surgery or advised to have surgery	___	___	_____
17. Taking medication regularly	___	___	_____
18. Allergies or skin problems	___	___	_____
19. Menstrual problems; LMP	___	___	_____

Signature _____ Date _____

Emergency Information Card

Athlete's name _____ Age _____

Address _____

Home phone _____ Cell phone _____

Sport _____

List two persons to contact in case of emergency:

Parent's or guardian's name _____ Home phone _____

Address _____ Work phone _____

Second person's name _____ Home phone _____

Address _____ Work phone _____

Relationship to athlete _____

Insurance co. _____ Policy no. _____

Physician's name _____ Phone _____

Are you allergic to any drugs? _____ If so, what? _____

Do you have any allergies (e.g., bee stings or dust)? _____

Do you have _____ asthma, _____ diabetes, or _____ epilepsy? (Check any that apply)

Do you take any medications? _____ If so, what? _____

Do you wear contact lenses? _____

Other _____

Signature _____ Date _____

Weather Emergency Plan

1. Weather decision maker. Who is responsible for deciding when to cease practices and competitions? Write that person's name here:

2. Specific criteria for when to suspend activities. Describe the conditions that would cause you to suspend sport activities due to the following types of weather.

   • Lightning: (For example, would athletes seek shelter if thunder occurs within 30 seconds of a lightning strike, or would just the occurrence of thunder, without lightning, be enough to stop activities?)

   • Hail, tornadoes, hurricanes, and damaging winds:

   • Extreme heat:

   • Extreme cold:

   • Winter weather (snow, ice):

3. Weather watcher. Who is responsible for monitoring weather reports for watches and warnings, and notifying the decision maker of serious weather conditions? Write that person's name here:

4. Method for monitoring weather conditions. How will you monitor weather conditions? For example, will you use a weather radio, or do you have access to a television weather station?

5. Designated safe place. Where will you seek shelter from these serious weather conditions?

   • Lightning:

   • Hail, tornadoes, hurricanes, and damaging winds:

6. Guidelines for resuming activity. Describe the specific criteria that have to be met before activity can resume (when the following weather conditions have been present).

   • Lightning: (For example, do not leave the shelter until 30 minutes after the last lightning strike or clap of thunder.)

   • Hail, tornadoes, hurricanes, and damaging winds:

   • Extreme heat:

   • Extreme cold:

   • Winter weather (snow, ice):

ACTIVITY 3.3

Disqualifying Medical Conditions

To test your knowledge of disqualifying medical conditions, complete the following table by placing a check mark in the correct column. If the presence of the condition may disqualify an athlete from participation, or limit an athlete's participation, place a check mark in the left-hand column. If it is generally okay for the athlete to play, even with the condition present, place a check mark in the right-hand column.

Condition	May disqualify the athlete or limit the athlete's participation	Generally okay to play
Uncontrolled diabetes		
Uncontrolled asthma		
Dental appliances		
Heart conditions		
Uncontrolled high blood pressure		
Athlete's foot		
Epilepsy		
Previous head injuries		
Previous spinal injuries		
Chronic orthopedic problems (e.g., unstable knees, ankles, or shoulders)		
Chronic allergies		
Athlete has been released by a physician after recovering from a broken ankle		
History of heat illness		

ACTIVITY 3.4

Getting Players Ready to Perform

Please specify true (T) or false (F) for each of the following statements about preseason physical exams, preseason screening, conditioning, and skill instruction.

_____ 1. Any health care worker can conduct preseason physical exams.

_____ 2. Athletes can turn in their physical exam forms any time during the season.

_____ 3. If a physician does not clear an athlete for participation, you can allow the athlete to practice, but not compete, with the team.

_____ 4. All health history forms should be kept in a confidential and secure file.

_____ 5. A physical exam will provide detailed information about an athlete's level of fitness.

_____ 6. Preseason screenings can be conducted by athletic trainers or certified strength and conditioning coaches.

_____ 7. Preseason screenings typically include evaluating athletes for strength, flexibility, endurance, cardiovascular endurance, body composition, and coordination.

_____ 8. Preseason screenings typically include vision and hearing screening.

_____ 9. Preseason screenings are used to pinpoint potential fitness problems and target conditioning exercises to improve these problem areas before the season.

_____ 10. Preseason conditioning can be started as late as two weeks before the start of the season.

_____ 11. Conditioning exercises should focus on muscle strength, endurance, flexibility, power, and speed.

_____ 12. Individual athletes may do different conditioning exercises depending on their sport, position, and fitness level.

_____ 13. To improve strength, athletes should perform three sets of 12 to 15 repetitions of each exercise, five days a week.

_____ 14. Well-supervised resistance training has proven safe for prepubescent athletes, but you can avoid weightlifting-related injuries by emphasizing body-weight-only exercises, such as push-ups.

_____ 15. Cardiovascular endurance can be improved by training three days a week for at least 20 continuous minutes.

_____ 16. Flexibility can be improved by stretching two days a week.

_____ 17. If an athlete is using an incorrect skill technique but is performing well, you should not correct the technique.

_____ 18. It is the district's responsibility to inform you of banned or injury-prone techniques, such as spearing in football or diving headfirst into a base in softball.

ACTIVITY 3.5

Warm-Up, Cool-Down, and Nutrition

Circle the correct answer for each multiple-choice question.

1. LaTonya is an outfielder on your softball team. Which of the following activities should be included at the beginning of her warm-up?

    a. wind sprints

    b. pitching

    c. light jogging

    d. rest periods

2. LaTonya, an outfielder on your softball team, is almost done with her workout. At the end of her workout, which of the following activities should be included in her cool-down?

    a. intense calisthenics

    b. throwing, batting, and fielding drills

    c. a sudden stop to exercising

    d. light jogging and stretching

3. The National Athletic Trainers' Association recommends that athletes drink this amount of fluid during workouts, practices, and competitions:

    a. 10 to 12 ounces of sports drink every 15 to 20 minutes

    b. 10 to 12 ounces of cool water every 15 to 20 minutes

    c. 7 to 10 ounces of cool water or sports drink every 20 to 30 minutes

    d. 7 to 10 ounces of cool water or sports drink every 10 to 20 minutes

4. Which statement best describes the amount of fluid that athletes should drink before and after workouts, practices, and competitions?

    a. Athletes should limit their fluid intake before activity sessions but drink plenty after exercising.

    b. Athletes should begin hydrating two hours before an activity session, and after the session they should drink 24 fluid ounces of water or sports drink for every pound of water lost through sweat.

    c. Athletes should drink plenty starting two hours before an activity session but limit their fluid intake after exercising.

    d. Athletes should focus on their fluid intake during an activity session and not worry about how much fluid they drink before or after exercising.

5. Most high school athletes should eat a diet _____.

    a. high in carbohydrate, moderate in protein, and low in fat

    b. moderate in carbohydrate, high in protein, and high in fat

    c. low in carbohydrate, moderate in protein, and moderate in fat

    d. low in carbohydrate, low in protein, and moderate in fat

6. According to the food guide pyramid, which one of the following food groups should athletes consume the least of?

    a. milk, yogurt, and cheese

    b. fats, oils, and sweets

    c. meat, eggs, and nuts

    d. bread, cereal, rice, and pasta

7. Which athlete is most likely to have an upset stomach during competition?

    a. Alecia, who ate plenty of high-carbohydrate foods before her competition

    b. Jessica, who ate a high-fat meal, including a large order of french fries, before her competition

    c. Luis, who ate three hours before his competition

    d. Tyler, who ate his favorite meal before his competition, even though the rest of his team ate Chinese food, which Tyler had never tried

ACTIVITY 3.6

Medical Emergency Plan

Note: This is an optional activity if you do not have a current coaching position.

In this activity, you will develop a medical emergency plan for your current coaching position. Write your plans on the Medical Emergency Plan on pages 79 to 81. You can then copy this plan and distribute it to those who need it.

Medical Emergency Plan

First, you need to prepare to respond to injuries.

1. Where will you keep the laminated Sport First Aid Quick Reference Card so that you can immediately refer to it when an athlete is injured?

2. _____ will be responsible for bringing the first aid kit to every practice and competition.

How Do I Assess an Injured Athlete?

These topics are covered in chapter 4 of *Sport First Aid,* and you learned about them in the classroom portion of the course.

1. *What to do first when you arrive at an injured athlete's side.* List the first steps you should take (from pages 50 and 52 of *Sport First Aid*). The first few entries are filled in for you.

   a. Assess the scene

   - Instruct others to leave the athlete alone.

   - Consider the environment.

   - _____

   - _____

   b. Assess the athlete.

   - Review how the injury or illness occurred and the athlete's medical history.

   - _____

   - _____

2. *How to attend to responsive and unresponsive athletes.* Explain the basic steps of responding to responsive and unresponsive athletes. (See pages 52 to 53 of *Sport First Aid.*)

   Responsive Athletes

   a.

   b.

   c.

   d.

   Unresponsive Athletes

   a.

   b.

   c.

   d.

(continued)

Medical Emergency Plan *(continued)*

How Do I Activate (Call) the EMS?

1. Delegate the responsibility of seeking medical help. The person can be an assistant coach, a parent, or an athlete. But it must be someone who is calm and responsible. Make sure that this person is on-hand before every practice and game.

    a. _____ will call for emergency medical assistance when it is needed for my team.

2. Write out a list of emergency telephone numbers.

    a. Write the following phone numbers here and transfer them to a list that you can place in your first aid kit:

    - Rescue unit _____

    - Hospital _____

    - Physician _____

    - Police _____

    - Fire department _____

    b. _____ will talk to the host coaches of away games about emergency services.

3. Take each athlete's emergency information card to every practice and game.

    a. _____ will be responsible for bringing copies of the athletes' emergency information cards to every practice and game.

    b. Have you made copies of the emergency information cards? If not, write a reminder here to do so.

4. Give an emergency response card to the contact person calling for emergency assistance.

5. Complete an injury report form and keep it on file for any injury that occurs.

    a. Where do you keep blank injury report forms?

    b. Who needs to receive a copy of any completed injury report forms?

    c. Where will you store copies of completed injury report forms for your own records?

How Will First Aid Care Be Provided?

Who Will Provide Care?

> If emergency medical assistance is not present, who has first responsibility for providing first aid care? Write a prioritized list of responders here, and communicate your expectations to the people involved. For example, your list may look like this: (1) athletic trainer (if present), (2) coach, (3) assistant coach.

Handling Minor Injuries

Using page 27 of *Sport First Aid,* write the list of steps to take when a minor injury occurs.

1.

2.

3.

4.

5.

6.

Handling Serious Injuries

Using page 27 of *Sport First Aid,* write the list of steps to take when a serious injury occurs.

1.

2.

3.

4.

5.

6.

7.

8.

ACTIVITY 3.3

Disqualifying Medical Conditions

Condition	May disqualify the athlete or limit the athlete's participation	Generally okay to play
Uncontrolled diabetes	X	
Uncontrolled asthma	X	
Dental appliances		X
Heart conditions	X	
Uncontrolled high blood pressure	X	
Athlete's foot		X
Epilepsy	X	
Previous head injuries	X	
Previous spinal injuries	X	
Chronic orthopedic problems (e.g., unstable knees, ankles, or shoulders)	X	
Chronic allergies		X
Athlete has been released by a physician after recovering from a broken ankle		X
History of heat illness	X	

ACTIVITY 3.4

Getting Players Ready to Perform

F   1. Any health care worker can conduct preseason physical exams. *(Preseason physical exams must be done by a physician.)*

F   2. Athletes can turn in their physical exam forms any time during the season. *(Physical exam forms must be turned in before the season begins.)*

F   3. If a physician does not clear an athlete for participation, you can allow the athlete to practice, but not compete, with the team. *(If a physician does not clear an athlete for participation, the athlete cannot practice or compete until released by the physician.)*

T   4. All health history forms should be kept in a confidential and secure file.

F   5. A physical exam will provide detailed information about an athlete's level of fitness. *(Preseason screening must be done to determine information about an athlete's level of fitness.)*

T   6. Preseason screenings can be conducted by athletic trainers or certified strength and conditioning coaches.

T   7. Preseason screenings typically include evaluating athletes for strength, flexibility, endurance, cardiovascular endurance, body composition, and coordination.

F   8. Preseason screenings typically include vision and hearing screening. *(Preseason screenings focus on physical fitness issues.)*

T   9. Preseason screenings are used to pinpoint potential fitness problems and target conditioning exercises to improve these problem areas before the season.

F 10. Preseason conditioning can be started as late as two weeks before the start of the season. *(Conditioning should be started six weeks before the season.)*

T 11. Conditioning exercises should focus on muscle strength, endurance, flexibility, power, and speed.

T 12. Individual athletes may do different conditioning exercises depending on their sport, position, and fitness level.

___F___   13. To improve strength, athletes should perform three sets of 12 to 15 repetitions of each exercise, five days a week. *(Two sets of 6 to 8 repetitions, three days a week, is recommended to increase strength.)*

___T___   14. Well-supervised resistance training has proven safe for prepubescent athletes, but you can avoid weightlifting-related injuries by emphasizing body-weight-only exercises, such as push-ups.

___T___   15. Cardiovascular endurance can be improved by training three days a week for at least 20 continuous minutes.

___F___   16. Flexibility can be improved by stretching two days a week. *(Stretching five days a week may be required to improve flexibility.)*

___F___   17. If an athlete is using an incorrect skill technique but is performing well, you should not correct the technique. *(Many athletes are injured because they use incorrect technique.)*

___F___   18. It is the district's responsibility to inform you of banned or injury-prone techniques, such as spearing in football or diving headfirst into a base in softball. *(It is the coach's responsibility to know and teach correct skill techniques.)*

ACTIVITY 3.5

Warm-Up, Cool-Down, and Nutrition

Correct answers appear in boldface type.

1. LaTonya is an outfielder on your softball team. Which of the following activities should be included at the beginning of her warm-up?
   a. wind sprints
   b. pitching
   C. LIGHT JOGGING
   d. rest periods

2. LaTonya, an outfielder on your softball team, is almost done with her workout. At the end of her workout, which of the following activities should be included in her cool-down?
   a. intense calisthenics

b. throwing, batting, and fielding drills

c. a sudden stop to exercising

D. LIGHT JOGGING AND STRETCHING

3. The National Athletic Trainers' Association recommends that athletes drink this amount of fluid during workouts, practices, and competitions:

   a. 10 to 12 ounces of sports drink every 15 to 20 minutes

   b. 10 to 12 ounces of cool water every 15 to 20 minutes

   c. 7 to 10 ounces of cool water or sports drink every 20 to 30 minutes

   D. 7 TO 10 OUNCES OF COOL WATER OR SPORTS DRINK EVERY 10 TO 20 MINUTES

4. Which statement best describes the amount of fluid that athletes should drink before and after workouts, practices, and competitions?

   a. Athletes should limit their fluid intake before activity sessions but drink plenty after exercising.

   B. ATHLETES SHOULD BEGIN HYDRATING TWO HOURS BEFORE AN ACTIVITY SESSION, AND AFTER THE SESSION THEY SHOULD DRINK 24 FLUID OUNCES OF WATER OR SPORTS DRINK FOR EVERY POUND OF WATER LOST THROUGH SWEAT.

   c. Athletes should drink plenty starting two hours before an activity session but limit their fluid intake after exercising.

   d. Athletes should focus on their fluid intake during an activity session and not worry about how much fluid they drink before or after exercising.

5. Most high school athletes should eat a diet _____.

   A. HIGH IN CARBOHYDRATE, MODERATE IN PRO- TEIN, AND LOW IN FAT

   b. moderate in carbohydrate, high in protein, and high in fat

   c. low in carbohydrate, moderate in protein, and moderate in fat

   d. low in carbohydrate, low in protein, and moderate in fat

6. According to the food guide pyramid, which one of the following food groups should athletes consume the least of?

   a. milk, yogurt, and cheese

   B. FATS, OILS, AND SWEETS

    c. meat, eggs, and nuts

    d. bread, cereal, rice, and pasta

7. Which athlete is most likely to have an upset stomach during competition?

    a. Alecia, who ate plenty of high-carbohydrate foods before her competition

    B. JESSICA, WHO ATE A HIGH-FAT MEAL, INCLUDING A LARGE ORDER OF FRENCH FRIES, BEFORE HER COMPETITION

    c. Luis, who ate three hours before his competition

    d. Tyler, who ate his favorite meal before his competition, even though the rest of his team ate Chinese food, which Tyler had never tried

ACTIVITY 3.6

Medical Emergency Plan

First, you need to prepare to respond to injuries.

1. Where will you keep the laminated Sport First Aid Quick Reference Card so that you can immediately refer to it when an athlete is injured? *[Your answer here]*

2. ___*[Your answer here]*___ will be responsible for bringing the first aid kit to every practice and competition.

How Do I Assess an Injured Athlete?

These topics are covered in chapter 4 of *Sport First Aid,* and you learned about them in the classroom portion of the course.

1. *What to do first when you arrive at an injured athlete's side.* List the first steps you should take (from pages 50 and 52 of *Sport First Aid*).

   a. Assess the scene.

   - Instruct others to leave the athlete alone.
   - Consider the environment.
   - Calm the athlete.
   - Check the athlete's position and equipment.

   b. Assess the athlete.

   - Review how the injury or illness occurred and the athlete's medical history.
   - Determine responsiveness.

2. *How to attend to responsive and unresponsive athletes.* Explain the basic steps of responding to responsive and unresponsive athletes. (See pages 52 to 53 of *Sport First Aid*.)

   Responsive Athletes

   a. Check airway: Athlete is talking and able to keep his or her airway open and clear.
   b. Check for breathing: The athlete is breathing normally.
   c. Check for severe bleeding: If severe bleeding is found, control immediately.
   d. Check circulation: Tissue color and body temperature are normal.

   Unresponsive Athlete

   a. Alert EMS or activate your Emergency Action Plan.
   b. Check the ABCs. Roll the athlete over if necessary to determine whether he or she is breathing normally.
   d. If athlete is not breathing normally or you're unsure, immediately give two rescue breaths.
   e. If athlete is not breathing normally after two rescue breaths, begin external chest compressions (give CPR).

(continued)

Medical Emergency Plan *(continued)*

How Do I Activate (Call) the EMS?

1. Delegate the responsibility of seeking medical help. The person can be an assistant coach, a parent, or an athlete. But it must be someone who is calm and responsible. Make sure that this person is on-hand before every practice and game.

   a. _[Your answer here]_____ will call for emergency medical assistance when it is needed for my team.

2. Write out a list of emergency telephone numbers.

   a. Write the following phone numbers here and transfer them to a list that you can place in your first aid kit:

      • Rescue unit _____

      • Hospital _____

      • Physician _____

      • Police _____

      • Fire department _____

   b. _[Your answer here]_____ will talk to the host coaches of away games about emergency services.

3. Take each athlete's emergency information card to every practice and game.

   a. _[Your answer here]_____ will be responsible for bringing copies of the athletes' emergency information cards to every practice and game.

   b. Have you made copies of the emergency information cards? If not, write a reminder here to do so.

4. Give an emergency response card to the contact person calling for emergency assistance.

5. Complete an injury report form and keep it on file for any injury that occurs.

   a. Where do you keep blank injury report forms?

      [Your answer here]

   b. Who needs to receive a copy of any completed injury report forms?

      [Your answer here]

   c. Where will you store copies of completed injury report forms for your own records?

      [Your answer here]

Medical Emergency Plan *(continued)*

How Will First Aid Care Be Provided?

Who Will Provide Care?

If emergency medical assistance is not present, who has first responsibility for providing first aid care? Write a prioritized list of responders here, and communicate your expectations to the people involved. For example, your list may look like this: (1) athletic trainer (if present), (2) coach, (3) assistant coach.

[Your answer here]

Handling Minor Injuries

Using page 27 of *Sport First Aid,* write the list of steps to take when a minor injury occurs.

1. Assess the injury.

2. Administer first aid.

3. Remove the athlete from participation if the athlete is in a great deal of pain or suffers from a loss of function (can't walk, run, jump, or throw).

4. Contact the athlete's parents to discuss the injury.

5. Suggest that the athlete see a physician to rule out a serious injury.

6. Complete an injury report form while the incident is still fresh in your mind.

Handling Serious Injuries

Using page 27 of *Sport First Aid,* write the list of steps to take when a serious injury occurs.

1. **Check** the athlete's level of responsiveness.

2. Send a contact person to **call** emergency medical personnel and the athlete's parents.

3. Send someone to wait for the rescue team, help them open doors and gates, and direct them to the injured athlete.

4. Assess **(check)** the injury.

5. Administer first aid **(care)**.

6. Assist emergency medical personnel in preparing the athlete for transportation to a medical facility.

7. Appoint someone to go with the athlete if the parents are not available. This person should be responsible, calm, and familiar with the athlete. Assistant coaches or parents are best for this job.

8. Complete an injury report form while the incident is still fresh in your mind.

Anatomy and Sport Injury Terminology

LEARNING OBJECTIVES

In this unit, you will learn

- what the roles of the musculoskeletal, neurological, digestive, circulatory and respiratory, and urinary systems are;
- how most injuries and illnesses occur;
- what distinguishes acute and chronic injuries; and
- how to recognize the main types of acute and chronic injuries.

WHAT TO READ

Read chapter 3, "Anatomy and Sport Injury Terminology," in *Sport First Aid.*

ACTIVITY 4.1

Features of the Body's Systems

Match the body system with its primary features. Write the letter of the features on the blank line next to the body system that best matches.

Body system	Features
____ 1. Musculoskeletal	a. Kidneys, ureter, and bladder
____ 2. Neurological	b. Esophagus, small and large intestines, liver, gallbladder, and pancreas
____ 3. Digestive	c. Heart, blood vessels, trachea, and lungs
____ 4. Circulatory and respiratory	d. Bones, joints, ligaments, cartilage, muscles, tendons, and bursas
____ 5. Urinary	e. Brain, spinal cord, and network of nerves

ACTIVITY 4.2

Systems and Anatomy

Circle the best answer for each multiple-choice question.

1. Which organ does not provide a fluid to aid the digestive process?
    a. liver
    b. appendix
    c. pancreas
    d. gallbladder

2. Oxygen is supplied to the body through the _____ system.
    a. musculoskeletal
    b. neurological
    c. digestive
    d. circulatory and respiratory

3. The urinary system begins its work when waste products in the blood are transferred into the _____.
    a. liver
    b. arteries
    c. kidneys
    d. pancreas

4. The vertebrae are held together by _____.
    a. nerves
    b. ligaments
    c. cartilage discs
    d. the spinal cord

5. Messages pass between the brain and nerves through the _____.
   a. synovial sheath
   b. cartilage discs
   c. spinal cord
   d. vertebrae

6. The place where two bones meet is called the _____.
   a. joint
   b. bursa
   c. rotator cuff
   d. synovial sheath

7. Bones are connected by _____.
   a. ligaments
   b. cartilage
   c. muscles
   d. tendons

8. The function of cartilage is to _____.
   a. absorb shock and reduce friction between bones
   b. connect bones to each other
   c. connect muscles to bones
   d. protect important organs

9. Small, fluid-filled sacs between bones and tendons are called _____.
   a. ligaments
   b. cartilage
   c. tendons
   d. bursas

10. The upper arm bone is held in the shoulder socket by the _____ muscles.
    a. gastrocnemius
    b. quadriceps
    c. rotator cuff
    d. hamstring

ACTIVITY 4.3

Identifying Anatomy

1. Write the name of the corresponding bone in each blank below.

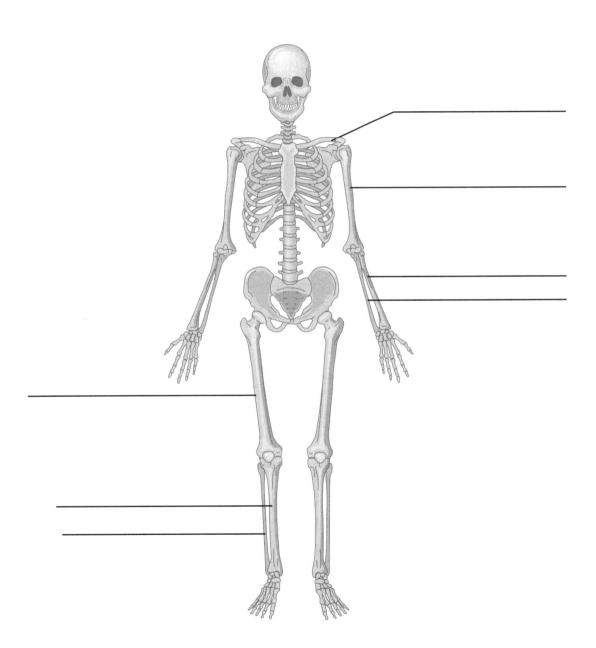

2. Write the name of the corresponding muscle group in each blank below.

3. Write the name of the corresponding tendon in each blank below.

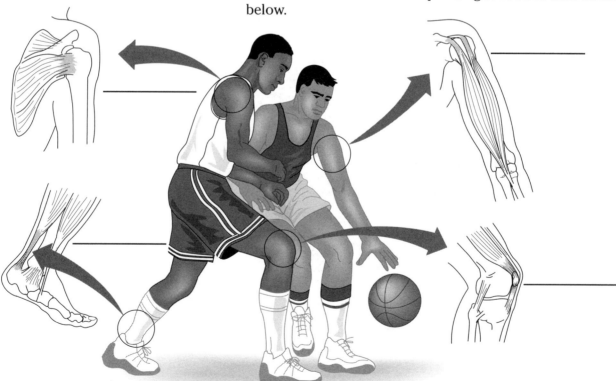

ACTIVITY 4.4

Acute Versus Chronic

For each of the following statements, write *Acute* in the blank if the statement refers to an acute injury or illness. Write *Chronic* if it refers to a chronic injury or illness.

_____ 1. These injuries occur suddenly as a result of a specific injury mechanism.

_____ 2. These injuries develop over a period of several weeks and are typically caused by repeated injury.

_____ 3. Shauna broke her radius when she stretched out her arm to brace for a fall.

_____ 4. David sprained his ankle and will be out for several weeks.

_____ 5. Lisa developed tennis elbow from using incorrect backhand technique.

_____ 6. Julie has asthma and must use an inhaler.

_____ 7. James went into anaphylactic shock after being stung by a bee.

ACTIVITY 4.5

Strains Versus Sprains

Circle the best answer for each multiple-choice question.

1. Strains occur in _____.
   a. ligaments
   b. muscles and tendons
   c. bones
   d. cartilage

2. Sprains occur in _____.
   a. ligaments
   b. muscles and tendons
   c. bones
   d. cartilage

3. In a Grade II strain or sprain, the injured part is _____.
   a. stretched slightly
   b. torn completely
   c. dislocated
   d. stretched and partially torn

4. A high jumper attempts to beat her personal best without warming up and partially tears her patellar tendon. This athlete has suffered a _____.

   a. Grade III sprain

   b. Grade I strain

   c. Grade II strain

   d. Grade III strain

5. A large center falls on the side of a running back's lower leg, tearing the running back's knee ligament completely. This athlete has suffered a _____.

   a. Grade III sprain

   b. Grade I strain

   c. Grade II strain

   d. Grade III strain

6. A basketball player stretches her Achilles tendon. This athlete has suffered a _____.

   a. Grade III sprain

   b. Grade I strain

   c. Grade II strain

   d. Grade III strain

7. A wrestler suffers a fully torn quadriceps during a heated match. This athlete has suffered a _____.

   a. Grade III sprain

   b. Grade I strain

   c. Grade II strain

   d. Grade III strain

ACTIVITY 4.1

Features of the Body's Systems

Body system	Features
__d__ 1. Musculoskeletal	d. Bones, joints, ligaments, cartilage, muscles, tendons, and bursas
__e__ 2. Neurological	e. Brain, spinal cord, and network of nerves
__b__ 3. Digestive	b. Esophagus, small and large intestines, liver, gallbladder, and pancreas
__c__ 4. Circulatory and respiratory	c. Heart, blood vessels, trachea, and lungs
__a__ 5. Urinary	a. Kidneys, ureter, and bladder

ACTIVITY 4.2

Systems and Anatomy

Correct answers appear in boldface type.

1. Which organ does not provide a fluid to aid the digestive process?
    a. liver
    B. APPENDIX
    c. pancreas
    d. gallbladder

2. Oxygen is supplied to the body through the _____ system.
    a. musculoskeletal
    b. neurological
    c. digestive
    D. CIRCULATORY AND RESPIRATORY

3. The urinary system begins its work when waste products in the blood are transferred into the _____.
    a. liver
    b. arteries
    C. KIDNEYS
    d. pancreas

4. The vertebrae are held together by _____.
   a. nerves
   B. LIGAMENTS
   c. cartilage discs
   d. the spinal cord

5. Messages pass between the brain and nerves through the _____.
   a. synovial sheath
   b. cartilage discs
   C. SPINAL CORD
   d. vertebrae

6. The place where two bones meet is called the _____.
   A. JOINT
   b. bursa
   c. rotator cuff
   d. synovial sheath

7. Bones are connected by _____.
   A. LIGAMENTS
   b. cartilage
   c. muscles
   d. tendons

8. The function of cartilage is to _____.
   A. ABSORB SHOCK AND REDUCE FRICTION BETWEEN BONES
   b. connect bones to each other
   c. connect muscles to bones
   d. protect important organs

9. Small, fluid-filled sacs between bones and tendons are called _____.
   a. ligaments
   b. cartilage
   c. tendons
   D. BURSAS

10. The upper arm bone is held in the shoulder socket by the _____ muscle.
    a. gastrocnemius
    b. quadriceps
    C. ROTATOR CUFF
    d. hamstring

ACTIVITY 4.3

Identifying Anatomy

1. Write the name of the corresponding bone in each blank below.

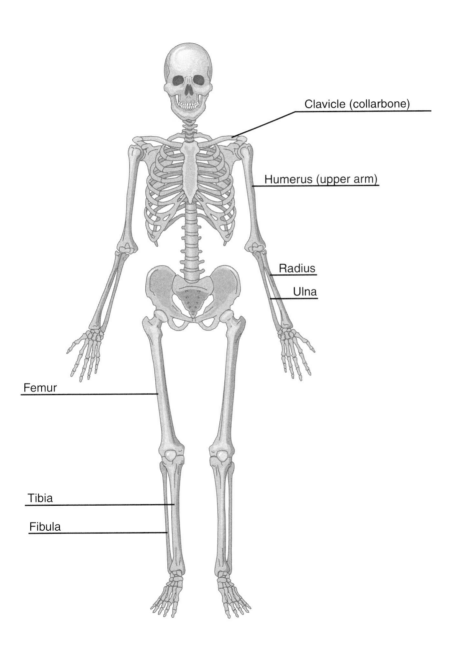

Clavicle (collarbone)

Humerus (upper arm)

Radius

Ulna

Femur

Tibia

Fibula

2. Write the name of the corresponding muscle group in each blank below.

Rotator cuff

Hamstrings

Calf (gastrocnemius)

Quadriceps

3. Write the name of the corresponding tendon in each blank below.

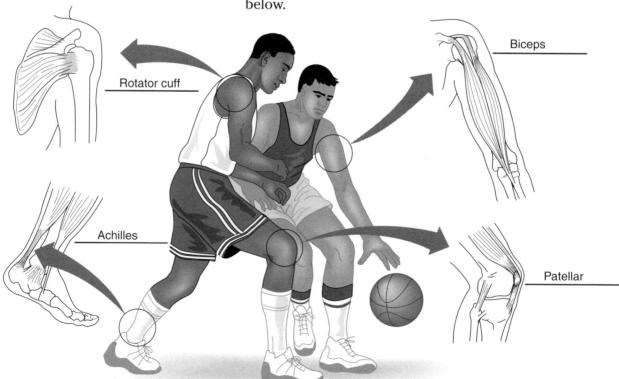

Rotator cuff

Biceps

Achilles

Patellar

ACTIVITY 4.4

Acute Versus Chronic

   Acute   1. These injuries occur suddenly as a result of a specific injury mechanism.

   Chronic 2. These injuries develop over a period of several weeks and are typically caused by repeated injury.

   Acute   3. Shauna broke her radius when she stretched out her arm to brace for a fall.

   Acute   4. David sprained his ankle and will be out for several weeks.

   Chronic 5. Lisa developed tennis elbow from using incorrect backhand technique.

   Chronic 6. Julie has asthma and must use an inhaler.

   Acute   7. James went into anaphylactic shock after being stung by a bee.

ACTIVITY 4.5

Strains Versus Sprains

Correct answers appear in boldface type.

1. Strains occur in _____.
   a. ligaments
   B. MUSCLES AND TENDONS
   c. bones
   d. cartilage

2. Sprains occur in _____.
   A. LIGAMENTS
   b. muscles and tendons
   c. bones
   d. cartilage

3. In a Grade II strain or sprain, the injured part is _____.
   a. stretched slightly
   b. torn completely
   c. dislocated
   D. STRETCHED AND PARTIALLY TORN

4. A high jumper attempts to beat her personal best without warming up and partially tears her patellar tendon. This athlete has suffered a _____.

    a. Grade III sprain

    b. Grade I strain

    C. GRADE II STRAIN

    d. Grade III strain

5. A large center falls on the side of a running back's lower leg, tearing the running back's knee ligament completely. This athlete has suffered a _____.

    A. GRADE III SPRAIN

    b. Grade I strain

    c. Grade II strain

    d. Grade III strain

6. A basketball player stretches her Achilles tendon. This athlete has suffered a _____.

    a. Grade III sprain

    B. GRADE I STRAIN

    c. Grade II strain

    d. Grade III strain

7. A wrestler suffers a fully torn quadriceps during a heated match. This athlete has suffered a _____.

    a. Grade III sprain

    b. Grade I strain

    c. Grade II strain

    D. GRADE III STRAIN

Emergency Action Steps and Providing Life Support

LEARNING OBJECTIVES

In this unit, you will learn

- what to do first when an athlete goes down due to an injury or illness;
- how to perform emergency action steps, which include checking if the athlete has an airway, is breathing, and has good circulation;
- what to do if an athlete is having trouble breathing, including how to perform cardiopulmonary resuscitation and how to use an automated external defibrillator;
- how to recognize and respond to an airway blockage, including how to perform the Heimlich maneuver.

WHAT TO READ

Read chapter 4, "Emergency Action Steps and Providing Life Support," in *Sport First Aid*.

ACTIVITY 5.1

Injury Scenario and Response

In this three-part activity, you will read about an injury that you encounter as a coach and then decide in what order you should perform the first aid steps.

▶ Part I Assessing the Scene and Assessing the Athlete ‑ ‑ ‑ ‑ ‑ ‑ ‑ ‑ ‑ ‑ ‑

During your first practice as a track team coach, you suddenly see that your star runner, Larry, is lying face down on the track. You didn't have a good view of what happened to him. Larry doesn't appear to be moving.

Based on the situation given in the scenario, number the following steps in the order that you should perform them. Three bogus steps are included, which should not be numbered.

_____ Move Larry off the track to protect him from further harm.

_____ Mentally review Larry's relevant medical history.

_____ Mentally review how the injury or illness occurred.

_____ Get him some water.

_____ Check whether his equipment or position will hinder your assessment and your ability to provide first aid care for a life-threatening condition.

_____ Shake Larry's shoulders vigorously.

_____ Determine whether Larry is responsive by calling out his name and tapping or squeezing his shoulder.

▶ Part II Alerting and Attending to the ABCs ‑ ‑ ‑ ‑ ‑ ‑ ‑ ‑ ‑ ‑ ‑ ‑ ‑ ‑ ‑ ‑

Larry, your star runner, is lying face down on the track after collapsing. You tap Larry's shoulder and ask "Are you all right, Larry?" Larry does not appear to be moving and is not responsive. You know that your next step is to check the ABCs.

Based on what you have learned from assessing the scene and athlete, number the following steps in the order that you should perform them. Three bogus steps are included, which should not be numbered.

_____ Send for emergency medical assistance and an AED, if an AED is available.

_____ Look, listen, and feel for breathing for 5, but no more than 10, seconds.

_____ Remove Larry's t-shirt.

_____ While you look, listen, and feel for breathing, check Larry's tissue color and temperature.

_____ Carry Larry off of the track.

_____ Roll Larry on his back and open his airway.

_____ Roll Larry on his side so that vomit can drain from his mouth.

▶ Part III Maintaining Life Support- -

After failing to feel or hear any breath from Larry's mouth or see his chest rise and fall, you ask your assistant to help you carefully roll him over so you will be in a position to give CPR if needed. Opening Larry's airway using the head tilt-chin lift does not produce any signs of breathing, and you notice his nail beds have a bluish tinge. You give Larry two rescue breaths, and his chest rises with each breath, so you know that his airway is not obstructed.

Based on what you have learned about maintaining basic life support, number the following steps in the order that you should perform them. For this scenario, assume that an AED becomes available after you have performed CPR for about 2 minutes. Three bogus steps are included, which should not be numbered.

_____ Wrap Larry in a blanket to keep him warm.

_____ Deliver 30 compressions in a row, pushing fast and hard.

_____ Give 5 cycles of 30 compressions and 2 rescue breaths.

_____ Kneel by Larry, positioning your hands and body to begin cardiopulmonary resuscitation (CPR).

_____ Perform the Heimlich maneuver.

_____ Place cool compresses on Larry's armpits and inner thighs.

_____ Turn on the AED and apply the pads. Allow the AED to analyze the heart rhythm and then follow the AED prompts.

_____ Give Larry 2 rescue breaths, making sure his chest rises with each breath.

ACTIVITY 5.1

Injury Scenario and Response

▶ *Part I Assessing the Scene and Assessing the Athlete* - - - - - - - - -

During your first practice as a track team coach, you suddenly see that your star runner, Larry, is lying face down on the track. You didn't have a good view of what happened to him. Larry doesn't appear to be moving.

Based on the situation given in the scenario, number the following steps in the order that you should perform them. Three bogus steps are included, which should not be numbered.

_____ Move Larry off the track to protect him from further harm.

__2__ Mentally review Larry's relevant medical history.

__1__ Mentally review how the injury or illness occurred.

_____ Get him some water.

__3__ Check whether his equipment or position will hinder your assessment and your ability to provide first aid care for a life-threatening condition.

_____ Shake Larry's shoulders vigorously.

__4__ Determine whether Larry is responsive by calling out his name and tapping or squeezing his shoulder.

▶ *Part II Alerting and Attending to the ABCs* - - - - - - - - - - - - - - -

Larry, your star runner, is lying face down on the track after collapsing. You tap Larry's shoulder and ask "Are you all right, Larry?" Larry does not appear to be moving and is not responsive. You know that your next step is to check the ABCs.

Based on what you have learned from assessing the scene and athlete, number the following steps in the order that you should perform them. Three bogus steps are included, which should not be numbered.

___1___ Send for emergency medical assistance and an AED, if an AED is available.

___3___ Look, listen, and feel for breathing for 5, but no more than 10, seconds.

_____ Remove Larry's t-shirt.

___4___ While you look, listen, and feel for breathing, check Larry's tissue color and temperature.

_____ Carry Larry off of the track.

___2___ Roll Larry on his back and open his airway.

_____ Roll Larry on his side so that vomit can drain from his mouth.

▶ Part III Maintaining Life Support

After failing to feel or hear any breath from Larry's mouth or see his chest rise and fall, you ask your assistant to help you carefully roll him over so you will be in a position to give CPR if needed. Opening Larry's airway using the head tilt-chin lift does not produce any signs of breathing, and you notice his nailbeds have a bluish tinge. You give Larry two rescue breaths, and his chest rises with each breath, so you know that his airway is not obstructed.

Based on what you have learned about maintaining basic life support, number the following steps in the order that you should perform them. For this scenario, assume that an AED becomes available after you have performed CPR for about 2 minutes. Three bogus steps are included, which should not be numbered.

_____ Wrap Larry in a blanket to keep him warm.

___2___ Deliver 30 compressions in a row, pushing fast and hard.

___4___ Give 5 cycles of 30 compressions and 2 rescue breaths.

___1___ Kneel by Larry, positioning your hands and body to begin cardiopulmonary resuscitation (CPR).

_____ Perform the Heimlich maneuver.

_____ Place cool compresses on Larry's armpits and inner thighs.

___5___ Turn on the AED and apply the pads. Allow the AED to analyze the heart rhythm and then follow the AED prompts.

___3___ Give Larry 2 rescue breaths, making sure his chest rises with each breath.

Physical Assessment and First Aid for Bleeding, Tissue Damage, and Unstable Injuries

LEARNING OBJECTIVES

In this unit, you will learn

- how to conduct a physical assessment of an injured or ill athlete using the HIT (history, inspection, and touch) method;
- how to control profuse bleeding;
- what methods to use to minimize widespread tissue damage;
- how to splint unstable injuries;
- how to control slow, steady bleeding; and
- what to do to minimize local tissue damage.

WHAT TO READ

Read chapter 5, "Physical Assessment and First Aid Techniques," in *Sport First Aid.*

ACTIVITY 6.1

Bleeding

▶ *Part I First Aid for Profuse Arterial and Venous Bleeding* - - - - - - - - -

Jamie strikes her wrist on the volleyball standard while diving for a save. She has a deep gash below the palm. You complete the emergency action steps and the physical assessment and identify Jamie's profusely bleeding wrist as the one injury requiring immediate attention.

Number the following steps in the order in which you should perform them to control Jamie's profuse bleeding.

_____ Send for emergency medical assistance.

_____ Apply firm, direct pressure over the wound with your hand.

_____ Cover the wound with sterile gauze pads.

_____ If initial dressings become soaked with blood, place additional gauze pads and roller qauze over the existing dressings.

_____ Put on gloves and goggles or a mask, if you haven't already done so, to protect yourself against blood-borne pathogens.

_____ Wash any portion of your skin that comes in contact with blood or body fluid; bag and then wash contaminated clothing; clean contaminated surfaces with a bleach solution; place contaminated gloves and bandages in a biohazard waste bag; and wash your hands after removing examination gloves.

_____ Use elastic roller gauze to secure the sterile gauze pads covering the wound.

_____ Monitor and treat for shock as needed.

_____ Monitor breathing and circulation and provide CPR as needed.

▶ *Part II First Aid for Slow, Capillary Bleeding* - - - - - - - - - - - - - - - - -

Jason gets tangled with another player as he goes up for a layup. He lands sideways on the court and slides on his left arm. After conducting the emergency action steps and physical assessment, you find that Jason is fortunate to have no serious injuries. The only injury you need to care for is a superficial skin abrasion on Jason's arm that is slowly oozing blood.

Number the following steps in the order in which you should perform them to control Jason's capillary bleeding.

_____ If you are unable to clean all debris from the wound, or if the wound edges gape open and do not touch (may need stitches), send the athlete to a physician.

_____ Apply sterile gauze, then firm, direct pressure over the wound with your hand.

_____ Once bleeding stops, gently clean the wound and cover it with sterile gauze or bandage.

_____ Put on gloves and goggles or a mask as needed, if you haven't already done so, to protect yourself against blood-borne pathogens.

_____ Wash any portion of your skin that comes in contact with blood or body fluid; bag and then wash contaminated clothing; clean contaminated surfaces with a bleach solution; place contaminated gloves and bandages in a biohazard waste bag; and wash your hands after removing examination gloves.

ACTIVITY 6.2

Tissue Damage

▶ *Part I Is It Shock or Local Tissue Damage?* - - - - - - - - - - - - - - - - - -

In the table on page 112, place a check mark in the "Shock" column if the signs or symptoms relate to the emergency situation of systemic tissue damage. Place a check mark in the "Local tissue damage" column if the signs or symptoms relate to a local tissue reaction.

Signs or symptoms	Shock	Local tissue damage
Fatigue		
Bruising at site of injury		
Weakness		
Dizziness		
Swelling around site of injury		
Temperature increase at site of injury		
Anxiety		
Pain at site of injury		
Thirst		
Nausea		
Inability to use a body part		
Cool and clammy skin		
Pale or grayish skin		
Weak and rapid pulse		
Slow and shallow breathing		
Dilated pupils		
Blank stare		
Confusion		
Possible unconsciousness		
Sweating		
Shaking or shivering		
Bluish lips and fingernails		

▶ Part II First Aid for Systemic Tissue Damage (Shock) - - - - - - - - - - -

Your forward, Teresa, collides with an opponent and seems to have a compound fracture of the ankle. She's lying flat on her back, and she's in a lot of pain. You've completed the emergency action steps and physical assessment, and she seems in no danger. However, you continue to pay attention to Teresa's breathing, and you notice that it has become slow and shallow.

You ask Teresa if she feels weak or dizzy. She says she does. She also sounds increasingly anxious and is starting to shiver. She says she's thirsty and requests a drink. You now know that you must provide first aid care for possible shock.

Number the following steps in the order in which you should perform them to minimize Teresa's shock response. One bogus step is included, which should not be numbered.

_____ Provide first aid care for bleeding and other injuries.

_____ Keep the athlete flat on her back.

_____ Send for emergency medical assistance if you haven't already done so.

_____ Give Teresa something to drink.

_____ Monitor breathing and provide CPR if needed.

_____ Maintain normal body temperature by covering the athlete as needed.

▶ Part III First Aid for Local Tissue Damage - - - - - - - - - - - - - - - - -

Chenna, a first-year tennis player, dives for a return and lands hard on his wrist. You perform the emergency action steps and find that Chenna's airway, breathing, and circulation are all fine. From the physical assessment, you find that Chenna has likely sustained a minor wrist sprain. You know that the best way to speed Chenna's recovery is to minimize the local tissue damage that may occur from the sprain.

Number the following steps in the order in which you should perform them to minimize Chenna's local tissue damage.

_____ Elevate Chenna's wrist above his heart.

_____ Immobilize the sprained wrist and prevent Chenna from doing any activity that causes pain.

_____ Apply an elastic wrap to his wrist.

_____ Place a bag of crushed ice on his wrist.

_____ Protect Chenna from further injury by preventing him from moving and by keeping other athletes and hazards clear of him.

ACTIVITY 6.1

Bleeding

▶ **Part I First Aid for Profuse Arterial and Venous Bleeding** - - - - - - - - -

Jamie strikes her wrist on the volleyball standard while diving for a save. She has a deep gash below the palm. You complete the emergency action steps and physical assessment and identify Jamie's profusely bleeding wrist as the one injury requiring immediate attention.

Number the following steps in the order in which you should perform them to control Jamie's profuse bleeding.

__2__ Send for emergency medical assistance.

__4__ Apply firm, direct pressure over the wound with your hand.

__3__ Cover the wound with sterile gauze.

__6*__ If initial dressings become soaked with blood, place additional gauze pads and roller gauze over the existing dressings.

__1__ Put on gloves and goggles or a mask, if you haven't already done so, to protect yourself against blood-borne pathogens.

__9__ Wash any portion of your skin that comes in contact with blood or body fluid; bag and then wash contaminated clothing; clean contaminated surfaces with a bleach solution; place contaminated gloves and bandages in a biohazard waste bag; and wash your hands after removing examination gloves.

__5*__ Use elastic roller gauze to secure the sterile gauze pads covering the wound.

__8__ Monitor and treat for shock as needed.

__7__ Monitor breathing and circulation and provide rescue breathing or CPR as needed.

* Steps 5 and 6 may be reversed; they may take place at the same decision point.

▶ *Part II First Aid for Slow, Capillary Bleeding* - - - - - - - - - - - - - - -

Jason gets tangled with another player as he goes up for a layup. He lands sideways on the court and slides on his left arm. After conducting the emergency action steps and the physical assessment, you find that Jason is fortunate to have no serious injuries. The only injury you need to care for is a superficial skin abrasion on Jason's arm that is slowly oozing blood.

Number the following steps in the order in which you should perform them to control Jason's capillary bleeding.

___4___ If you are unable to clean all debris from the wound, or if the wound edges gape open and do not touch (may need stitches), send the athlete to a physician.

___2___ Apply sterile gauze, then firm, direct pressure over the wound with your hand.

___3___ Once bleeding stops, gently clean the wound and cover it with sterile gauze or bandage.

___1___ Put on gloves and goggles or a mask as needed, if you haven't already done so, to protect yourself against blood-borne pathogens.

___5___ Wash any portion of your skin that comes in contact with blood or body fluid; bag and then wash contaminated clothing; clean contaminated surfaces with a bleach solution; place contaminated gloves and bandages in a biohazard waste bag; and wash your hands after removing examination gloves.

ACTIVITY 6.2

Tissue Damage

► **Part I Is It Shock or Local Tissue Damage?**- - - - - - - - - - - - - - - - - -

Signs or symptoms	Shock	Local tissue damage
Fatigue	X	
Bruising at site of injury		X
Weakness	X	
Dizziness	X	
Swelling around site of injury		X
Temperature increase at site of injury		X
Anxiety	X	
Pain at site of injury		X
Thirst	X	
Nausea	X	
Inability to use a body part		X
Cool and clammy skin	X	
Pale or grayish skin	X	
Weak and rapid pulse	X	
Slow and shallow breathing	X	
Dilated pupils	X	
Blank stare	X	
Confusion	X	
Possible unconsciousness	X	
Sweating	X	
Shaking or shivering	X	
Bluish lips and fingernails	X	

▶ Part II First Aid for Systemic Tissue Damage (Shock) - - - - - - - - - - -

Your forward, Teresa, collides with an opponent and seems to have a compound fracture of the ankle. She's lying flat on her back, and she's in a lot of pain. You've completed the emergency action steps and the physical assessment, and she seems in no danger. However, you continue to pay attention to Teresa's breathing, and you notice that it has become slow and shallow. You ask Teresa if she feels weak or dizzy. She says she does. She also sounds increasingly anxious and is starting to shiver. She says she's thirsty and requests a drink. You now know that you must provide first aid care for possible shock.

Number the following steps in the order in which you should perform them to minimize Teresa's shock response. One bogus step is included, which should not be numbered.

__5__ Provide first aid care for bleeding and other injuries.

__2__ Keep the athlete flat on her back.

__1__ Send for emergency medical assistance if you haven't already done so.

_____ Give Teresa something to drink.

__3__ Monitor breathing and circulation and provide CPR if needed.

__4__ Maintain normal body temperature by covering the athlete as needed.

▶ Part III First Aid for Local Tissue Damage - - - - - - - - - - - - - - - - -

Chenna, a first-year tennis player, dives for a return and lands hard on his wrist. You perform the emergency action steps and find that Chenna's airway, breathing, and circulation are all fine. From the physical assessment, you find that Chenna has likely sustained a minor wrist sprain. You know that the best way to speed Chenna's recovery is to minimize the local tissue damage that may occur from the sprain.

Number the following steps in the order in which you should perform them to minimize Chenna's local tissue damage.

__5__ Elevate Chenna's wrist above his heart.

__2__ Immobilize the sprained wrist and prevent Chenna from doing any activity that causes pain.

__4__ Apply an elastic wrap to his wrist.

__3__ Place a bag of crushed ice on his wrist.

__1__ Protect Chenna from further injury by preventing him from moving and by keeping other athletes and hazards clear of him.

Moving Injured or Sick Athletes

LEARNING OBJECTIVES

In this unit, you will learn

- when to call for emergency medical assistance to move an athlete;
- when it may be acceptable to move an athlete yourself;
- what moving techniques you should use; and
- how to do the four- or five-person rescue, the one-person drag, the one-person walking assist, the two-person walking assist, the four-handed carrying assist, and the two-handed carrying assist.

WHAT TO READ

Read chapter 6, "Moving Injured or Sick Athletes," in *Sport First Aid.*

ACTIVITY 7.1

Selecting the Best Method for Moving an Athlete

Read each injury scenario, and answer the questions that follow.

▶ Scenario 1 -

During practice, a player on your soccer team has twisted her knee and dislocated her kneecap. She cannot step down on the injured leg, but she's all the way down the field from the bench at the far goal. You and your assistant are the only adults available to move the injured athlete.

    1. Should you move the athlete?

    2. If so, which moving technique should you use?

▶ Scenario 2 -

An athlete is punched in the face by an angry teammate, resulting in a fractured eye socket.

    1. Should you move this athlete?

    2. If so, which moving technique should you use?

▶ Scenario 3 -

One of your volleyball players twists her ankle during practice. She is able to put some pressure on the ankle, but she needs support to get back to the bench. You are the only adult present.

    1. Should you move this athlete?

    2. If so, which moving technique should you use?

▶ Scenario 4 -

Two basketball players collide in midair. One falls hard to the ground. She is lying on her stomach and is unresponsive. You cannot tell if she is breathing. Several coaches are present.

1. Should you move this athlete?

2. If so, which moving technique should you use?

▶ Scenario 5 -

An athlete has a badly strained calf muscle and is unable to walk or support his own weight. A parent offers to help move the athlete.

1. Should you move this athlete?

2. If so, which moving technique should you use?

► *Scenario 6* -

Your football players are walking from the practice field back to the school building. It has been a grueling morning, with high humidity and temperatures reaching 95 degrees Fahrenheit. You look back to check the field and notice that one of your players is lying still on the ground. Although you offered plenty of water breaks, you knew that this player had been struggling with the heat. In fact, you had asked him to sit out several times. As you run toward the collapsed player, you recall no event that would have caused any type of injury. When you reach him, you find that he is breathing but not responsive. His breathing is rapid, and his skin is hot and flushed. You suspect that he is suffering from heatstroke. Your ice water immersion tub is filled and too heavy to lift. It is 10 yards away from the collapsed athlete. By now everyone else is back at the school building, and you are the only person present.

1. Should you move this athlete?

2. If so, which moving technique should you use?

ACTIVITY 7.1

Selecting the Best Method for Moving an Athlete

Scenario 1 -

During practice, a player on your soccer team has twisted her knee and dislocated her kneecap. She cannot step down on the injured leg, but she's all the way down the field from the bench at the far goal. You and your assistant are the only adults available to move the injured athlete.

1. Should you move the athlete?

Yes. you can move this athlete safely and should not allow her to walk on the injured leg.

2. If so, which moving technique should you use?

Because you have to move the athlete a long distance and there are only two of you to support her, use the four-handed carrying assist.

Scenario 2 -

An athlete is punched in the face by an angry teammate, resulting in a fractured eye socket.

1. Should you move this athlete?

No. A fractured eye socket is considered a critical injury, and the athlete should not be moved. You should call for emergency medical assistance to transport the athlete.

2. If so, which moving technique should you use?

You would not move this athlete because the athlete is critically injured.

Scenario 3 -

One of your volleyball players twists her ankle during practice. She is able to put some pressure on the ankle, but she needs support to get back to the bench. You are the only adult present.

    1. Should you move this athlete?

Yes. It is safe to move this athlete because she is not critically injured.

    2. If so, which moving technique should you use?

The one-person walking assist.

Scenario 4 -

Two basketball players collide in midair. One falls hard to the ground. She is lying on her stomach and is unresponsive. You cannot tell if she is breathing. Several coaches are present.

    1. Should you move this athlete?

Yes. Even though this athlete may be critically injured, you need to roll her on her back to check for breathing and to provide first aid care.

    2. If so, which moving technique should you use?

The four- or five-person rescue should be used to turn the athlete on her back as a unit.

Scenario 5 -

An athlete has a badly strained calf muscle and is unable to walk or support his own weight. A parent offers to help move the athlete.

    1. Should you move this athlete?

Yes. It is safe to move this athlete because he is not critically injured.

    2. If so, which moving technique should you use?

The two-handed carrying assist should be used because the athlete cannot support his own weight and two adults are present to help move the athlete.

▶ Scenario 6 -

Your football players are walking from the practice field back to the school building. It has been a grueling morning, with high humidity and temperatures reaching 95 degrees Fahrenheit. You look back to check the field and notice that one of your players is lying still on the ground. Although you offered plenty of water breaks, you knew that this player had been struggling with the heat. In fact, you had asked him to sit out several times. As you run toward the collapsed player, you recall no event that would have caused any type of injury. When you reach him, you find that he is breathing but not responsive. His breathing is rapid, and his skin is hot and flushed. You suspect that he is suffering from heatstroke. Your ice water immersion tub is filled and too heavy to lift. It is 10 yards away from the collapsed athlete. By now everyone else is back at the school building, and you are the only person present.

1. Should you move this athlete?

Yes. This athlete must be quickly cooled with water and ice.

2. If so, which moving technique should you use?

The one-person drag should be used because you are the only person present and the athlete must be cooled quickly.

Respiratory Emergencies and Illnesses

LEARNING OBJECTIVES

In this unit, you will learn

- how to identify the signs and symptoms of anaphylactic shock, asthma, collapsed lung, throat contusion, pneumonia or bronchitis, solar plexus spasm ("wind knocked out"), and hyperventilation;

- what first aid care to provide for each of these conditions; and

- how to prevent allergies, asthma, bronchitis, and pneumonia from progressing into life-threatening emergencies.

WHAT TO READ

Read chapter 7, "Respiratory Emergencies and Illnesses," in *Sport First Aid.*

ACTIVITY 8.1

Responding to Respiratory Emergencies

Instructions

1. Review each of the scenarios and identify the causes, symptoms, and signs of the injury described in the scenario.

2. For each scenario, complete the following steps, using *Sport First Aid* as a reference:

   a. In the Causes, Symptoms, and Signs table on page 127, find the column that lists information for the injury described in the scenario. Write the injury name and scenario name (e.g., "Scenario 2, Ashley") at the top of the appropriate column.

   b. In the First Aid table on page 128, find the column that shows the steps to take for the injury described in the scenario, and write the injury name and scenario name at the top of the appropriate column.

▶ Scenario 1, Yanmei -

Yanmei is taking a break on the bench when the play on the basketball court gets rough. A player falls, and the player's elbow hits hard into Yanmei's chest. Yanmei grabs her chest in pain and gasps for air. You rush to her side and quickly perform the emergency action steps. Yanmei's breathing is rapid. In your physical assessment, you recall where Yanmei got hit and ask Yanmei where it hurts. She holds her chest, over her rib cage. You inspect the area and see a small bruise quickly forming. Her ribs don't look right to you. When you touch the area, you can feel that the ribs are broken and pushed backward.

▶ Scenario 2, Ashley -

Your soccer team is practicing, and you notice that play has stopped and that Ashley is standing still, struggling to catch her breath. You run to her aid and find that she can't seem to get a good breath. A fellow teammate tells you that Ashley got hit in the stomach by the ball, and by asking questions you find that she got hit just below her rib cage. When you ask Ashley where it hurts, she points to the area just below her breastbone.

▶ Scenario 3, Daniel -

In a surprising turn of events, Daniel, one of your pitchers, gets grazed in the throat by a baseball. You immediately change pitchers. As Daniel comes to the dugout, you can tell something is wrong. You quickly assess Daniel's airway, breathing, and circulation and find that his breathing is quite rapid. You think through how the injury occurred and inspect the area where Daniel was hit, finding swelling and discoloration. When you touch the area, you hear a crunching sound.

Causes, Symptoms, and Signs Table

Injury name:	Injury name:	Injury name:
Scenario name:	Scenario name:	Scenario name:
Cause • Direct blow to the area below the rib cage	**Causes** • Direct blow to the ribs that compresses or tears the lung • Spontaneous collapse of a lung, not caused by an injury • Puncture by a sharp object such as a broken rib, an arrow, or a javelin	**Cause** • Direct blow to the throat area (e.g., getting hit with a baseball, softball, or hockey puck, or getting hit by an elbow in basketball or football)
Symptoms • Inability to breathe in (inhale) • Pain just below the breastbone	**Symptoms** • Shortness of breath • Chest pain	**Symptoms** • Pain in the throat • Pain with swallowing • Shortness of breath
Signs • Possible temporary unresponsiveness • Labored breathing or hyperventilation	**Signs** • Bruise or open wound in the chest • Sucking noise coming from an open chest wound • Gasping for air • Increased breathing rate	**Signs** • Gasping for air • Breathing rate may increase • Swelling or discoloration where the object hit the throat • Deformity in the throat area • Crunchy or grating sound when touched • Voice changes—may vary from hoarseness to total inability to speak • Difficulty swallowing • Wheezing • Coughing • Coughing up or spitting blood

First Aid Table

Injury name:	Injury name:	Injury name:
_____	_____	_____
Scenario name:	Scenario name:	Scenario name:
_____	_____	_____

First Aid	**First Aid**	**First Aid**
1. Reassure the athlete.	1. Reassure the athlete.	1. Send for emergency medical assistance.
2. Place the athlete in a seated or semireclining position.	2. Loosen constricting clothing.	2. Reassure the athlete.
3. Apply ice to the injured area to help reduce swelling.	3. Encourage the athlete to relax.	3. Place the athlete in a semireclining position as long as this doesn't cause further injury.
4. Monitor breathing and provide CPR if needed (if CPR is needed, send for medical assistance).	4. Instruct the athlete to take a short breath followed by a slow, deep breath.	4. Cover any open, sucking wound with a nonporous material such as aluminum foil or multiple layers of sterile gauze.
5. Within a few minutes, if breathing does not return to normal levels, or if the athlete's throat is swollen or deformed and the athlete is having difficulty talking or swallowing, send for medical assistance.	5. Monitor breathing and provide CPR if needed (if CPR is needed, send for medical assistance).	5. Monitor breathing and provide CPR if needed.
6. Treat for shock as needed and send for medical assistance if it occurs.	6. If the athlete still has pain or does not recover in a few minutes, call for emergency medical assistance.	
	7. Monitor for signs and symptoms of other internal injuries. Signs and symptoms to watch for include shock, vomiting, or coughing up blood.	

ACTIVITY 8.1
Responding to Respiratory Emergencies

Causes, Symptoms, and Signs Table

Injury name:	Injury name:	Injury name:
Solar plexus spasm (wind knocked out)	*Collapsed lung*	*Throat contusion*
Scenario name:	**Scenario name:**	**Scenario name:**
Scenario 2, Ashley	*Scenario 1, Yanmei*	*Scenario 3, Daniel*
Cause • Direct blow to the area below the rib cage	**Causes** • Direct blow to the ribs that compresses or tears the lung • Spontaneous collapse of a lung, not caused by an injury • Puncture by a sharp object such as a broken rib, an arrow, or a javelin	**Cause** • Direct blow to the throat area (e.g., getting hit with a baseball, softball, or hockey puck, or getting hit by an elbow in basketball or football)
Symptoms • Inability to breathe in (inhale) • Pain just below the breastbone	**Symptoms** • Shortness of breath • Chest pain	**Symptoms** • Pain in the throat • Pain with swallowing • Shortness of breath
Signs • Possible temporary unresponsiveness • Labored breathing or hyperventilation	**Signs** • Bruise or open wound in the chest • Sucking noise coming from an open chest wound • Gasping for air • Increased breathing rate	**Signs** • Gasping for air • Breathing rate may increase • Swelling or discoloration where the object hit the throat • Deformity in the throat area • Crunchy or grating sound when touched • Voice changes—may vary from hoarseness to total inability to speak • Difficulty swallowing • Wheezing • Coughing • Coughing up or spitting blood

First Aid Table

Injury name: _Throat contusion_	Injury name: _Solar plexus spasm (wind knocked out)_	Injury name: _Collapsed lung_
Scenario name: _Scenario 3, Daniel_	Scenario name: _Scenario 2, Ashley_	Scenario name: _Scenario 1, Yanmei_
First Aid 1. Reassure the athlete. 2. Place the athlete in a seated or semireclining position. 3. Apply ice to the injured area to help reduce swelling. 4. Monitor breathing and provide CPR if needed (if CPR is needed, send for medical assistance). 5. Within a few minutes, if breathing does not return to normal levels, or if the athlete's throat is swollen or deformed and the athlete is having difficulty talking or swallowing, send for medical assistance. 6. Treat for shock as needed and send for medical assistance if it occurs.	**First Aid** 1. Reassure the athlete. 2. Loosen constricting clothing. 3. Encourage the athlete to relax. 4. Instruct the athlete to take a short breath followed by a slow, deep breath. 5. Monitor breathing and provide CPR if needed (if CPR is needed, send for medical assistance). 6. If the athlete still has pain or does not recover in a few minutes, call for emergency medical assistance. 7. Monitor for signs and symptoms of other internal injuries. Signs and symptoms to watch for include shock, vomiting, or coughing up blood.	**First Aid** 1. Send for emergency medical assistance. 2. Reassure the athlete. 3. Place the athlete in a semireclining position as long as this doesn't cause further injury. 4. Cover any open, sucking wound with a nonporous material such as aluminum foil or multiple layers of sterile gauze. 5. Monitor breathing and provide CPR if needed.

Closed Head and Spine Injuries

LEARNING OBJECTIVES

In this unit, you will learn

- how to recognize the signs and symptoms of head and spine injuries,
- what first aid care to provide for both responsive and unresponsive athletes with head or spine injuries, and
- what head and spine injury prevention strategies you can incorporate into your sport first aid game plan.

WHAT TO READ

Read chapter 8, "Closed Head and Spine Injuries," in *Sport First Aid.*

ACTIVITY 9.1

Responding to Closed Head and Spine Injuries

Instructions

1. Review each of the scenarios and identify the causes, symptoms, and signs of the injury described in the scenario.

2. For each scenario, complete the following steps, using *Sport First Aid* as a reference:

    a. In the Causes, Symptoms, and Signs table on pages 134 to 135, find the column that lists information for the injury described in the scenario. Write the injury name and scenario name (e.g., "Scenario 2, Jason") at the top of the appropriate column.

    b. In the First Aid table on pages 136 to 137, find the column that shows the steps to take for the injury described in the scenario, and write the injury name and scenario name at the top of the appropriate column.

▶ Scenario 1, Aden -

Aden hits his head on the goalpost during an intense soccer practice. He sits up after several seconds, seems a bit confused and unsteady, but insists that he is fine. You quickly perform the emergency action steps and find that his breathing is normal. In your physical assessment, you recall that Aden hit his head. You don't see any obvious bruising or external injury. You ask Aden if he feels dizzy. He reluctantly nods "yes" and says that he has a headache.

▶ Scenario 2, Jason -

At a preseason football practice, you notice your tight end, Jason, get up slowly and rub his neck awkwardly after taking an unexpected tackle from the left side. His breathing is normal, but he tells you that he felt an electrical shock sensation in his neck and left shoulder. He is experiencing slight numbness in his left hand and is unable to squeeze your fingers with full strength.

▶ Scenario 3, Jennifer- -

Jennifer hit her head on the balance beam when performing a dismount. She is lying on the mat, unresponsive. Her breathing is irregular. She has a bump on her head where she hit the beam. Her pupils do not constrict to light, and her pulse is irrregular.

▶ Scenario 4, Terrell

In a football game against a tough opponent, a play ends with players piled on top of one another. The players unravel themselves and stand up, but Terrell remains motionless on the ground. You quickly ascertain that his breathing and pulse are irregular. You didn't see how Terrell got injured, so you ask the other players what happened. They tell you that he got hit in his back by a helm…ent, fumbled the ball, and then fell to the ground. That's when everyone piled on, trying to recover the fumble. You take a closer look and see that there is clear fluid leaking from Terrell's ears.

▶ Scenario 5, Heather

Heather, one of your softball players, seems preoccupied after getting a base hit. The first base coach motions you over. You ask Heather what is wrong. She says she just doesn't feel right. Her back hurts. You ask her if she feels any numbness, and she replies that her left leg and foot are tingly. She also reports a sharp pain down the back of the same leg. You notice weakness in her foot when you ask her to push her foot against your hand.

Causes, Symptoms, and Signs Table

Injury name:	Injury name:	Injury name:
_____	_____	_____
Scenario name:	Scenario name:	Scenario name:
_____	_____	_____
Cause • Typically occurs when the head is turned or forced quickly to one side and tilted down	**Causes** • Direct blow • Compression • Torsion or twisting	**Causes** • Direct blow to the head • Sudden, forceful jarring or whipping of the head
Symptoms • Tingling or burning in the neck, shoulder, or arm • Electrical shock sensation	**Symptoms** • None can be ascertained	**Symptoms** • Dizziness • Slight ringing in the ears • Mild headache
Signs • Arm or hand numbness on one side—ask the athlete to name the finger that you are touching • Arm or hand weakness on one side—have the athlete squeeze your fingers with each hand	**Signs** • Athlete's responsiveness—if unresponsive, assume a head injury as well • Irregular breathing • Pulse irregularties • Profuse bleeding • Blood or fluid leaking from the mouth, nose, or ears • Spine deformity (if another trained rescuer can check without moving the athlete)	**Sign** • Slight, transient confusion

Injury name: _____	**Injury name:** _____
Scenario name: _____	**Scenario name:** _____
Causes • Direct blow • Compression • Torsion or twisting	**Causes** • Direct blow to the head • Sudden, forceful jarring or whipping of the head
Symptoms • Numbness or tingling in the toes, feet, fingers, or hands—ask the athlete to name the finger or toe that you are touching • Pain on or near the spine	**Symptoms** • None can be ascertained
Signs • Breathing irregularities • Pulse irregularities • Shock • Spine deformity—observed or touched (if another trained rescuer can check without moving the athlete) • Blood or clear fluid draining from the athlete's nose, mouth, or ears • Profuse bleeding caused by a collision or fall • Inability to move the fingers or toes • Grossly unequal handgrip strength—have the athlete try to squeeze your fingers • Unable to push toes or foot against your hand • Muscle spasms near the spine	**Signs** • Unresponsiveness to stimuli—Ask the athlete "Are you OK, (athlete's name)?" and tap on the shoulder. • Irregular breathing • Pulse irregularities • Bleeding or a wound at the point of the blow • Blood or fluid leaking from the nose or ears • Convulsions or seizures • Pupil abnormalities—unequal in size or fail to constrict to light • Deformity at the point of a direct blow • Eyes fail to uniformly track a moving object, such as your finger • Marked confusion or disorientation • Loss of balance • Slurred speech • Grogginess

First Aid Table

Injury name: _____ Scenario name: _____	Injury name: _____ Scenario name: _____	Injury name: _____ Scenario name: _____
First Aid 1. Protect the athlete from further harm: remove from activity. 2. Assign someone to monitor the athlete for symptoms and signs of severe injury. If such signs occur, send for emergency medical assistance. 3. For suspected mild concussion, notify the parents. Ask them to monitor the athlete, and give them a checklist of head injury signs and symtoms. Instruct them to take the athlete to a physician.	**First Aid** If any of the signs and symptoms are present, assume there is a serious spine injury. 1. Send for emergency medical assistance. 2. Stabilize the athlete's head and spine. 3. Monitor breathing and circulation and provide CPR if needed. 4. Control any profuse bleeding. 5. Monitor and treat for shock as needed. 6. If another trained rescuer is available, have that person manually stabilize any injured extremity. 7. Assist emergency medical personnel as needed.	**First Aid** 1. Send for emergency medical assistance. 2. Manually stabilize the athlete's head and neck. 3. Monitor breathing and circulation and provide CPR if needed. 4. Control any profuse bleeding. 5. Monitor and treat for shock as needed. 6. If another trained rescuer is available, have that person manually stabilize any injured extremity. 7. Assist emergency medical personnel as needed.

Injury name:

_____

Scenario name:

_____

First Aid

1. Contact emergency personnel immediately and assume that the athlete may also have a spine injury.
2. Manually stabilize the athlete's head and neck.
3. Monitor breathing and circulation and provide CPR if needed.
4. Control any profuse bleeding. If bleeding at the site of the injury, avoid excess pressure over the wound, especially if you notice a skull deformity or bone fragments.
5. Monitor and treat for shock as needed.
6. If another trained rescuer is available, have that person manually stabilize any injured extremity.
7. Assist emergency medical personnel as needed.

Injury name:

_____

Scenario name:

_____

First Aid

If sensation and strength do not return within five minutes, or there is tenderness or deformity of the spine, do the following:

1. Send for emergency medical assistance.
2. Manually stabilize the athlete's head and neck.
3. Monitor breathing and circulation and provide CPR if needed.
4. Monitor and treat for shock as needed.
5. If another trained rescuer is available, have that person manually stabilize any injured extremity.
6. Assist emergency medical personnel as needed.

ACTIVITY 9.1

Responding to Closed Head and Spine Injuries

Causes, Symptoms, and Signs Table

Injury name: Burner or stinger Scenario name: Scenario 2, Jason	Injury name: Unresponsive athlete with a spine injury Scenario name: Scenario 4, Terrell	Injury name: Mild concussion in a responsive athlete Scenario name: Scenario 1, Aden
Cause • Typically occurs when the head is turned or forced quickly to one side and tilted down	**Causes** • Direct blow • Compression • Torsion or twisting	**Causes** • Direct blow to the head • Sudden, forceful jarring or whipping of the head
Symptoms • Tingling or burning in the neck, shoulder, or arm • Electrical shock sensation	**Symptoms** • None can be ascertained	**Symptoms** • Dizziness • Slight ringing in the ears • Mild headache
Signs • Arm or hand numbness on one side—ask the athlete to name the finger that you are touching • Arm or hand weakness on one side—have the athlete squeeze your fingers with each hand	**Signs** • Athlete's responsiveness—if unresponsive, assume a head injury as well • Irregular breathing • Pulse irregularties • Profuse bleeding • Blood or fluid leaking from the mouth, nose, or ears • Spine deformity (if another trained rescuer can check without moving the athlete)	**Sign** • Slight, transient confusion

Injury name: *Responsive athlete with a spine injury*	**Injury name:** *Unresponsive athlete with a closed head injury (severe concussion)*
Scenario name: *Scenario 5, Heather*	**Scenario name:** *Scenario 3, Jennifer*
Causes • Direct blow • Compression • Torsion or twisting	**Causes** • Direct blow to the head • Sudden, forceful jarring or whipping of the head
Symptoms • Numbness or tingling in the toes, feet, fingers, or hands—ask the athlete to name the finger or toe that you are touching • Pain on or near the spine	**Symptoms** • None can be ascertained
Signs • Breathing irregularities • Pulse irregularities • Shock • Spine deformity—observed or touched (if another trained rescuer can check without moving the athlete) • Blood or clear fluid draining from the athlete's nose, mouth, or ears • Profuse bleeding caused by a collision or fall • Inability to move the fingers or toes • Grossly unequal handgrip strength—have the athlete try to squeeze your fingers • Unable to push toes or foot against your hand • Muscle spasms near the spine	**Signs** • Unresponsiveness to stimuli—Ask the athlete "Are you OK, (athlete's name)?" and tap on the shoulder. • Irregular breathing • Pulse irregularities • Bleeding or a wound at the point of the blow • Blood or fluid leaking from the nose or ears • Convulsions or seizures • Pupil abnormalities—unequal in size or fail to constrict to light • Deformity at the point of a direct blow • Eyes fail to uniformly track a moving object, such as your finger • Marked confusion or disorientation • Loss of balance • Slurred speech • Grogginess

First Aid Table

Injury name: _Mild concussion in a responsive athlete_ **Scenario name:** _Scenario 1, Aden_	Injury name: _Responsive athlete with a spine injury_ **Scenario name:** _Scenario 5, Heather_	Injury name: _Unresponsive athlete with a spine injury_ **Scenario name:** _Scenario 4, Terrell_
First Aid 1. Protect the athlete from further harm: remove from activity. 2. Assign someone to monitor the athlete for symptoms and signs of severe injury. If such signs occur, send for emergency medical assistance. 3. For suspected mild concussion, notify the parents. Ask them to monitor the athlete, and give them a checklist of head injury signs and symtoms. Instruct them to take the athlete to a physician.	**First Aid** If any of the signs and symptoms are present, assume there is a serious spine injury. 1. Send for emergency medical assistance. 2. Stabilize the athlete's head and spine. 3. Monitor breathing and circulation and provide CPR if needed. 4. Control any profuse bleeding. 5. Monitor and treat for shock as needed. 6. If another trained rescuer is available, have that person manually stabilize any injured extremity. 7. Assist emergency medical personnel as needed.	**First Aid** 1. Send for emergency medical assistance. 2. Manually stabilize the athlete's head and neck. 3. Monitor breathing and circulation and provide CPR if needed. 4. Control any profuse bleeding. 5. Monitor and treat for shock as needed. 6. If another trained rescuer is available, have that person manually stabilize any injured extremity. 7. Assist emergency medical personnel as needed.

Injury name:	Injury name:
Unresponsive athlete with a closed head injury (severe concussion)	*Burner or stinger*
Scenario name:	**Scenario name:**
Scenario 3, Jennifer	*Scenario 2, Jason*

First Aid

1. Contact emergency personnel immediately and assume that the athlete may also have a spine injury.
2. Manually stabilize the athlete's head and neck.
3. Monitor breathing and circulation and provide CPR if needed.
4. Control any profuse bleeding. If bleeding at the site of the injury, avoid excess pressure over the wound, especially if you notice a skull deformity or bone fragments.
5. Monitor and treat for shock as needed.
6. If another trained rescuer is available, have that person manually stabilize any injured extremity.
7. Assist emergency medical personnel as needed.

First Aid

If sensation and strength do not return within five minutes, or there is tenderness or deformity of the spine, do the following:

1. Send for emergency medical assistance.
2. Stabilize the head and neck.
3. Monitor breathing and circulation and provide CPR if needed.
4. Monitor and treat for shock as needed.
5. Stabilize any other unstable injuries.
6. Assist emergency medical personnel as needed.

Internal Organ Injuries

LEARNING OBJECTIVES

In this unit, you will learn

- how to recognize when an athlete has an internal injury, such as a ruptured spleen, bruised kidney, or testicular trauma;

- how to discern whether an athlete is in an early or an advanced, life-threatening stage of an internal organ injury;

- how to care for the injured athlete while waiting for emergency medical assistance;

- what to monitor if an athlete is exhibiting minor signs of an internal injury; and

- what information to give the parents of an athlete who has incurred an internal organ injury.

WHAT TO READ

Read chapter 9, "Internal Organ Injuries," in *Sport First Aid.*

ACTIVITY 10.1

Responding to Internal Organ Injuries

Instructions

1. Review each of the scenarios and identify the causes, symptoms, and signs of the injury described in the scenario.

2. For each scenario, complete the following steps, using *Sport First Aid* as a reference:

    a. In the Causes, Symptoms, and Signs table on page 145, find the column that lists information for the injury described in the scenario. Write the injury name and scenario name (e.g., "Scenario 2, Ben") at the top of the appropriate column.

    b. In the First Aid table on page 146, find the column that shows the steps to take for the injury described in the scenario, and write the injury name and scenario name at the top of the appropriate column.

▶ Scenario 1, Anthony -

During a football game with a fierce rival, Anthony takes a hard hit on his left side. Another player is shoved into Anthony and unintentionally rams Anthony with his helmet just underneath Anthony's stomach and lower ribs. Despite the tough competition, you pull Anthony out of the game, knowing you need to monitor him to make sure he is okay. You ask one of your assistant coaches to stand by Anthony on the sidelines. A couple plays later, your assistant calls you over. He and Anthony have sat down, and Anthony looks pale. You quickly check his breathing and find that he's short of breath. You ask Anthony how he feels, and he responds that he's a little dizzy. You ask him if it hurts anywhere. Anthony thinks for a moment and tells you that his left shoulder and neck hurt.

▶ Scenario 2, Ben- -

Your shortstop, Ben, gets hit hard in the groin with the baseball. The team laughs and groans with Ben in pain, but you know to take this more seriously. You take Ben out of the game to recover and give him an ice pack to put on the injury. A few minutes later, you can tell that Ben is still in pain, and you ask him how he feels. He says he's fine except for the pain. His breathing is normal. You encourage Ben to take slow, deep breaths and to continue to ice the injured area. You explain to Ben and his parents the possible injury, and you explain how to identify whether it is a more serious injury that requires physician attention.

▶ Scenario 3, Kelsey -

Kelsey gets kicked in the midback by another soccer player. You substitute a player for Kelsey so that she can take a break on the sidelines. At first Kelsey's breathing is normal. You can tell she'll have a good-sized bruise, and her midback hurts where she got kicked, but nothing else seems amiss. You ask a parent to sit with Kelsey for a few minutes. When you check back in, you find that Kelsey feels faint and her heart rate has increased. You ask Kelsey if it hurts anywhere else, and she gestures to her lower back, telling you the pain has spread down her back.

Causes, Symptoms, and Signs Table

Injury name: _____ Scenario name: _____	Injury name: _____ Scenario name: _____	Injury name: _____ Scenario name: _____
Cause • Direct blow to either side of the midback	**Cause** • A direct blow to the left side of the body, underneath the stomach and lower ribs	**Cause** • A direct blow to the groin area
Symptoms Early stage: • Pain at the site of the blow Advanced (life-threatening) stage: • Pain moves to the low back, outside thighs, or front pelvic area • Feels faint • Dizziness	**Symptoms** Early stage: • Pain in the left upper abdominal area Advanced (life-threatening) stage: • Pain progresses to the left shoulder or neck • Feels faint • Dizziness	**Symptoms** • Pain • Nausea
Signs Early stage: • Bruise or abrasion • Tenderness over the injured area Advanced (life-threatening) stage: • Abdominal swelling • Increased heart rate • Frequent and burning urination • Cloudy or bloody urine • Vomiting • Rigid back muscles over the injury site • Skin cool to touch • Pale skin	**Signs** Early stage: • Tenderness over left upper abdominal area • Abrasion or bruise over injured area Advanced (life-threatening) stage: • Pale skin • Rapid pulse • Vomiting • Rigid abdominal muscles • Low blood pressure • Shortness of breath	**Signs** For all cases: • Have athlete perform a self-exam, looking for swelling, discoloration, and deformity • Spasm of testicles Advanced stage: • Testicles draw upward • Bloody or cloudy urine • Vomiting

First Aid Table

Injury name:	Injury name:	Injury name:
_____	_____	_____
Scenario name:	Scenario name:	Scenario name:
_____	_____	_____
First Aid	**First Aid**	**First Aid**
1. Assist the athlete into a position that feels the most comfortable.	1. Send for emergency medical assistance if the initial signs and symptoms do not stop within a few minutes or if they progress to the advanced stages.	1. Send for emergency medical assistance if the initial symptoms and signs last longer than a few minutes or progress to the advanced stages.
2. Encourage the athlete to take slow, deep breaths.	2. Monitor breathing and provide CPR if needed (if CPR is needed, send for emergency medical assistance).	2. Monitor breathing and provide CPR if needed (if CPR is needed, send for emergency medical assistance).
3. Apply ice to the area for 15 minutes.	3. Monitor and treat for shock as needed and send for emergency medical assistance if it occurs.	3. Monitor and treat for shock as needed and send for emergency medical assistance if it occurs.
4. If the pain does not stop after 20 minutes, if the testicles draw upward, if the athlete has bloody or cloudy urine, or if the testicles exhibit swelling, discoloration, or tenderness more than an hour after the injury occurred (Koester 2000), notify the athlete's parents to take him to a physician.	4. Treat other injuries as needed.	4. Treat other injuries, such as possible rib fractures.
5. If the athlete recovers within a few minutes, notify the athlete's parents and explain how to identify signs and symptoms of a more severe injury (bloody or cloudy urine; testicles draw upward; or testicles exhibit swelling, discoloration, or tenderness).	5. If signs and symptoms do not progress to the advanced stages, but pain over the bruised area persists for more than 15 minutes, call the athlete's parents or guardian to take the athlete to a physician.	5. If signs and symptoms do not progress to the advanced stages, but tenderness over the upper abdominal area persists for more than 15 minutes, call the athlete's parents or guardian to take the athlete to a physician.
	6. If symptoms and signs disappear within a few minutes, notify the athlete's parents or guardian and explain how to identify signs and symptoms of a more severe injury.	6. If symptoms and signs disappear within a few minutes, notify the athlete's parents or guardian and explain how to identify signs and symptoms of a more severe injury.

ACTIVITY 10.1

Responding to Internal Organ Injuries

Causes, Symptoms, and Signs Table

Injury name: *Bruised kidney* Scenario name: *Scenario 3, Kelsey*	Injury name: *Ruptured spleen* Scenario name: *Scenario 1, Anthony*	Injury name: *Testicular trauma* Scenario name: *Scenario 2, Ben*
Cause • Direct blow to either side of the midback	**Cause** • A direct blow to the left side of the body, underneath the stomach and lower ribs	**Cause** • A direct blow to the groin area
Symptoms Early stage: • Pain at the site of the blow Advanced (life-threatening) stage: • Pain moves to the low back, outside thighs, or front pelvic area • Feels faint • Dizziness	**Symptoms** Early stage: • Pain in the left upper abdominal area Advanced (life-threatening) stage: • Pain progresses to the left shoulder or neck • Feels faint • Dizziness	**Symptoms** • Pain • Nausea
Signs Early stage: • Bruise or abrasion • Tenderness over the injured area Advanced (life-threatening) stage: • Abdominal swelling • Increased heart rate • Frequent and burning urination • Cloudy or bloody urine • Vomiting • Rigid back muscles over the injury site • Skin cool to touch • Pale skin	**Signs** Early stage: • Tenderness over left upper abdominal area • Abrasion or bruise over injured area Advanced (life-threatening) stage: • Pale skin • Rapid pulse • Vomiting • Rigid abdominal muscles • Low blood pressure • Shortness of breath	**Signs** For all cases: • Have athlete perform a self-exam, looking for swelling, discoloration, and deformity • Spasm of testicles Advanced stage: • Testicles draw upward • Bloody or cloudy urine • Vomiting

First Aid Table

Injury name: Testicular trauma	Injury name: Bruised kidney	Injury name: Ruptured spleen
Scenario name: Scenario 2, Ben	Scenario name: Scenario 3, Kelsey	Scenario name: Scenario 1, Anthony
First Aid 1. Assist the athlete into a position that feels the most comfortable. 2. Encourage the athlete to take slow, deep breaths. 3. Apply ice to the area for 15 minutes. 4. If the pain does not stop after 20 minutes, if the testicles draw upward, if the athlete has bloody or cloudy urine, or if the testicles exhibit swelling, discoloration, or tenderness more than an hour after the injury occurred (Koester 2000), notify the athlete's parents to take him to a physician. 5. If the athlete recovers within a few minutes, notify the athlete's parents and explain how to identify signs and symptoms of a more severe injury (bloody or cloudy urine; testicles draw upward; or testicles exhibit swelling, discoloration, or tenderness).	**First Aid** 1. Send for emergency medical assistance if the initial signs and symptoms do not stop within a few minutes or if they progress to the advanced stages. 2. Monitor breathing and provide CPR if needed (if CPR is needed, send for emergency medical assistance). 3. Monitor and treat for shock as needed and send for emergency medical assistance if it occurs. 4. Treat other injuries as needed. 5. If signs and symptoms do not progress to the advanced stages, but pain over the bruised area persists for more than 15 minutes, call the athlete's parents or guardian to take the athlete to a physician. 6. If symptoms and signs disappear within a few minutes, notify the athlete's parents or guardian and explain how to identify signs and symptoms of a more severe injury.	**First Aid** 1. Send for emergency medical assistance if the initial symptoms and signs last longer than a few minutes or progress to the advanced stages. 2. Monitor breathing and provide CPR if needed (if CPR is needed, send for emergency medical assistance). 3. Monitor and treat for shock as needed and send for emergency medical assistance if it occurs. 4. Treat other injuries, such as possible rib fractures. 5. If signs and symptoms do not progress to the advanced stages, but tenderness over the upper abdominal area persists for more than 15 minutes, call the athlete's parents or guardian to take the athlete to a physician. 6. If symptoms and signs disappear within a few minutes, notify the athlete's parents or guardian and explain how to identify signs and symptoms of a more severe injury.

REFERENCE

Koester, M.C. 2000. Initial evaluation and management of acute scrotal pain. *Journal of Athletic Training* 35(1): 76-79.

Sudden Illnesses

LEARNING OBJECTIVES

In this unit, you will learn

- how to recognize when an athlete is having a diabetic emergency and how to provide first aid care,
- how to recognize the signs and symptoms of grand mal and petit mal seizures,
- how to recognize adverse reactions to drugs and supplements,
- how to prevent and provide first aid care for fainting,
- how to recognize the signs and symptoms of influenza,
- how to recognize the signs and symptoms of gastroenteritis, and
- how to prevent influenza and gastroenteritis from spreading among your athletes.

WHAT TO READ

Read chapter 10, "Sudden Illnesses," in *Sport First Aid*.

ACTIVITY 11.1

Responding to Sudden Illnesses

Instructions

1. Review each of the scenarios and identify the causes, symptoms, and signs of the illness described in the scenario.

2. For each scenario, complete the following steps, using *Sport First Aid* as a reference:

   a. In the Causes, Symptoms, and Signs table on pages 152 to 153, find the column that lists information for the illness described in the scenario. Write the illness name and scenario name (e.g., "Scenario 2, Jim") at the top of the appropriate column.

   b. In the First Aid table on pages 154 to 155, find the column that shows the steps to take for the illness described in the scenario, and write the illness name and scenario name at the top of the appropriate column.

▶ *Scenario 1, Laura-* -

Minutes before taking the field for a game, you hear several athletes calling for help, and you notice the members of your team standing in a circle on the field and looking down. You rush over to find out what has happened and see Laura, your goalie, lying on the ground, her body convulsing. Laura's eyes are open, but her body appears rigid as her muscles contract violently. She is not responsive. You ask Laura's teammates what they saw, and they say that Laura was not injured in any way. She simply collapsed suddenly and started convulsing.

▶ *Scenario 2, Jim* -

Jim, the center fielder on your baseball team, has diabetes. During practice one afternoon, you notice that Jim is trembling slightly and sweating, even though it's a cool day. You ask him if everything is all right, and he seems impatient and asks you to leave him alone. You feel his radial pulse, and it's stronger and faster than you expected.

▶ Scenario 3, Keisha -

Your gymnastics team has been practicing hard for an upcoming competition. You know that some of the girls have been pushing themselves hard, though you have tried to be a voice of balance. As you gather the team for a prepractice talk, Keisha slumps against the vault, and a few of the girls catch her and gently help her to the floor. She is responsive, but her breathing is shallow and rapid. Her skin is cool and clammy. You ask Keisha to tell you how she feels. She says that she's tired and feels dizzy. She complains of a slight headache.

▶ Scenario 4, Dwayne -

Dwayne, a middle linebacker, has always been pumped up for football practice. Lately, though, he seems unusually full of energy, moody, and restless. At practice, these characteristics seem particularly marked, and you decide to check into things. You call Dwayne over and check his pulse. It's racing. You notice that his skin feels warm and his pupils are dilated.

▶ Scenario 5, Sarah -

Sarah shows up at basketball practice with a cough and a runny nose. When you get closer to her, you can see that her eyes are watery. You ask her how she feels, and Sarah tells you that she feels awful. She's achy and has a headache. You feel her forehead and guess that she has a fever.

Causes, Symptoms, and Signs Table

Illness name: _____ Scenario name: _____	Illness name: _____ Scenario name: _____	Illness name: _____ Scenario name: _____
Cause • Using a stimulant or taking an excessive amount of a stimulant	**Cause** • Respiration of the virus or direct contact with the virus	**Cause** • Usually brought on by extreme fatigue, dehydration, low blood pressure, or illness
Symptoms • Lack of fatigue • Irritability • Confusion • Mood changes • Feeling of hyperstimulation • Sense of mental clarity • Restlessness • Anxiety	**Symptoms** • Muscle or joint achiness • Headache • Fatigue	**Symptoms** • Nausea • Weakness • Headache • Fatigue • Dizziness
Signs • Dilated pupils • Increased body temperature • Rapid pulse • Hallucinations • Paranoia (high doses of cocaine) • Cardiac arrest (extreme cases)	**Signs** • Fever • Dry cough • Nasal congestion • Sore throat • Runny nose • Watery eyes	**Signs** • Pale, cool, clammy skin • Possibly shallow and rapid breathing • Possible loss of responsiveness

Illness name:	Illness name:
Scenario name:	Scenario name:

Causes	**Cause**
• Epilepsy	• High insulin levels, which may result from medications taken to control blood glucose levels
• Head injuries	
• Brain infection or tumor	
• Drug abuse	
• Respiratory arrest	
• High fever	
• Heatstroke	
• Hypoglycemia	
• Drug reactions	
• Medication discontinuation	

Symptoms	**Symptom**
• None can be ascertained	Mild:
	• Hunger

Signs	**Signs**
Minor/petit mal seizures:	Mild:
• Dazed or inattentive manner	• Irritability
• Confusion	• Slight weakness
• Loss of coordination	
• Possibly loss of speech	Moderate:
• Repetitive blinking or other small movements	• Dilated pupils
• Typically, these seizures are brief, lasting only seconds. However, some people may have many bouts in a day.	• Trembling
	• Sweating
Major/grand mal seizures (typical sequence):	• Strong, rapid pulse
• Eyes are generally open	Severe:
• Body appears stiff or rigid	• Confusion
• Muscles contract violently in spasms or convulsions that usually stop in one to two minutes	• Convulsions
• May temporarily stop breathing or appear to not be breathing, and progress to deep breathing after the seizure	• Unresponsiveness
• Bluish skin or lips	
• Unresponsiveness, followed by gradual return to responsiveness	
• Uncontrolled urination during the seizure	
• Temporary confusion after the seizure	

First Aid Table

Illness name:	Illness name:	Illness name:
Scenario name:	Scenario name:	Scenario name:
First Aid Mild to moderate: 1. Remove the athlete from all activity. 2. Give the athlete sugar, candy, pop, or fruit juice. 3. Send for emergency medical assistance if the athlete does not recover within a few minutes or signs progress to severe. 4. Monitor breathing and provide CPR if needed. 5. Inform the athlete's parents or guardian. Severe: 1. Send for emergency medical assistance. 2. Place an unresponsive athlete in the recovery position (if uninjured) or HAINES position (if injured) to allow vomit or fluids to drain from the mouth. 3. Monitor breathing and provide CPR if needed.	**First Aid** 1. Rest the athlete from all activity. 2. Encourage the athlete to drink plenty of liquids.	**First Aid** Minor/petit mal seizures: 1. Monitor for possible progression into grand mal seizure. 2. Rest the athlete from activity. 3. Inform the athlete's parents or guardian. Grand mal seizures: 1. Clear all objects away from the athlete. 2. Do not restrain the athlete. 3. Do not try to place anything in the athlete's mouth or try to pry the teeth apart. 4. After the convulsions stop, check breathing and provide CPR if needed. 5. Check for other possible injuries or illnesses if the athlete is not an epileptic. 6. If no suspected head or spine injuries, place the athlete in recovery position (if uninjured) or HAINES position (if injured) to allow fluids to drain from the mouth. 7. Monitor and treat for shock as needed and send for emergency medical assistance if it occurs. 8. Call the parents or guardian if the athlete is known to have epilepsy and recovers within a few minutes. 9. If the athlete is suffering from an injury or illness, is experiencing seizure for the first time, has a prolonged epileptic seizure (more than 5 minutes), has prolonged confusion or unresponsiveness (more than 10-15 minutes), has difficulty breathing, or is not an epileptic, you should send for emergency medical assistance. 10. Encourage the athlete to rest.

Illness name:	Illness name:
Scenario name:	Scenario name:
First Aid	**First Aid**
If athlete is responsive:	1. Rest the athlete from all activity.
1. Instruct the athlete to either sit (on a chair or bench) with head between knees, or lie down with feet elevated.	2. Send for emergency medical assistance if the symptoms don't improve or if the athlete goes into respiratory or cardiac arrest.
2. Monitor and treat for shock as needed and send for emergency medical assistance if it occurs.	3. Monitor breathing and provide CPR if needed.
3. If the athlete does not recover within a few minutes, send for emergency medical assistance.	4. Place an unresponsive athlete in the recovery position (if uninjured) or HAINES position (if injured) to allow fluids or vomit to drain from the mouth.
If athlete is unresponsive:	5. Treat for shock if necessary and send for emergency medical assistance if it occurs.
1. Monitor breathing and provide CPR if needed.	6. If the athlete recovers quickly, speak to the parents and send the athlete to a physician.
2. Send for emergency medical assistance if the athlete does not recover within a few minutes.	
3. Place athlete in recovery position (if uninjured) or HAINES position (if injured), not on back, to allow fluids to drain from the mouth.	
4. Monitor and treat for shock as needed and send for emergency medical assistance if it occurs.	

ACTIVITY 11.1

Responding to Sudden Illnesses

Causes, Symptoms, and Signs Table

Illness name: Stimulant reaction	Illness name: Influenza	Illness name: Fainting
Scenario name: Scenario 4, Dwayne	Scenario name: Scenario 5, Sarah	Scenario name: Scenario 3, Keisha
Cause • Using a stimulant or taking an excessive amount of a stimulant	**Cause** • Respiration of the virus or direct contact with the virus	**Cause** • Usually brought on by extreme fatigue, dehydration, low blood pressure, or illness
Symptoms • Lack of fatigue • Irritability • Confusion • Mood changes • Feeling of hyperstimulation • Sense of mental clarity • Restlessness • Anxiety	**Symptoms** • Muscle or joint achiness • Headache • Fatigue	**Symptoms** • Nausea • Weakness • Headache • Fatigue • Dizziness
Signs • Dilated pupils • Increased body temperature • Rapid pulse • Hallucinations • Paranoia (high doses of cocaine) • Cardiac arrest (extreme cases)	**Signs** • Fever • Dry cough • Nasal congestion • Sore throat • Runny nose • Watery eyes	**Signs** • Pale, cool, clammy skin • Possibly shallow and rapid breathing • Possible loss of responsiveness

Illness name:	Illness name:
Grand mal seizure	*Insulin reaction*
Scenario name:	**Scenario name:**
Scenario 1, Laura	*Scenario 2, Jim*

Causes	Cause
• Epilepsy	• High insulin levels, which may result from medications taken to control blood glucose levels
• Head injuries	
• Brain infection or tumor	
• Drug abuse	
• Respiratory arrest	
• High fever	
• Heatstroke	
• Hypoglycemia	
• Drug reactions	
• Medication discontinuation	

Symptoms	Symptom
• None can be ascertained	Mild:
	• Hunger

Signs	Signs
Minor/petit mal seizures:	Mild:
• Dazed or inattentive manner	• Irritability
• Confusion	• Slight weakness
• Loss of coordination	
• Possibly loss of speech	Moderate:
• Repetitive blinking or other small movements	• Dilated pupils
• Typically, these seizures are brief, lasting only seconds. However, some people may have many bouts in a day.	• Trembling
	• Sweating
Major/grand mal seizures (typical sequence):	• Strong, rapid pulse
• Eyes are generally open	
• Body appears stiff or rigid	Severe:
• Muscles contract violently in spasms or convulsions that usually stop in one to two minutes	• Confusion
	• Convulsions
• May temporarily stop breathing or appear to not be breathing, and progress to deep breathing after the seizure	• Unresponsiveness
• Bluish skin or lips	
• Unresponsiveness, followed by gradual return to responsiveness	
• Uncontrolled urination during the seizure	
• Temporary confusion after the seizure	

First Aid Table

Illness name:	Illness name:	Illness name:
Insulin reaction	*Influenza*	*Grand mal seizure*
Scenario name:	**Scenario name:**	**Scenario name:**
Scenario 2, Jim	*Scenario 5, Sarah*	*Scenario 1, Laura*

First Aid

Mild to moderate:

1. Remove the athlete from all activity.
2. Give the athlete sugar, candy, pop, or fruit juice.
3. Send for emergency medical assistance if the athlete does not recover within a few minutes or signs progress to severe.
4. Monitor breathing and provide CPR if needed.
5. Inform the athlete's parents or guardian.

Severe:

1. Send for emergency medical assistance.
2. Place an unresponsive athlete in the recovery position (if uninjured) or HAINES position (if injured) to allow vomit or fluids to drain from the mouth.
3. Monitor breathing and provide CPR if needed.

First Aid

1. Rest the athlete from all activity.
2. Encourage the athlete to drink plenty of liquids.

First Aid

Minor/petit mal seizures:

1. Monitor for possible progression into grand mal seizure.
2. Rest the athlete from activity.
3. Inform the athlete's parents or guardian.

Grand mal seizures:

1. Clear all objects away from the athlete.
2. Do not restrain the athlete.
3. Do not try to place anything in the athlete's mouth or try to pry the teeth apart.
4. After the convulsions stop, check breathing and provide CPR if needed.
5. Check for other possible injuries or illnesses if the athlete is not an epileptic.
6. If no suspected head or spine injuries, place the athlete in the recovery position (if uninjured) or HAINES position (if injured) to allow fluids to drain from the mouth.
7. Monitor and treat for shock as needed and send for emergency medical assistance if it occurs.
8. Call the parents or guardian if the athlete is known to have epilepsy and recovers within a few minutes.
9. If the athlete is suffering from an injury or illness, is experiencing seizure for the first time, has a prolonged epileptic seizure (more than 5 minutes), has prolonged confusion or unresponsiveness (more than 10-15 minutes), has difficulty breathing, or is not an epileptic, you should send for emergency medical assistance.
10. Encourage the athlete to rest.

Illness name: _Fainting_	Illness name: _Stimulant reaction_
Scenario name: _Scenario 3, Keisha_	Scenario name: _Scenario 4, Dwayne_
First Aid If athlete is responsive: 1. Instruct the athlete to either sit (on a chair or bench) with head between knees, or lie down with feet elevated. 2. Monitor and treat for shock as needed and send for emergency medical assistance if it occurs. 3. If the athlete does not recover within a few minutes, send for emergency medical assistance. If athlete is unresponsive: 1. Monitor breathing and provide CPR if needed. 2. Send for emergency medical assistance if the athlete does not recover within a few minutes. 3. Place athlete in the recovery position (if uninjured) or HAINES position (if injured), not on back, to allow fluids to drain from the mouth. 4. Monitor and treat for shock as needed and send for emergency medical assistance if it occurs.	**First Aid** 1. Rest the athlete from all activity. 2. Send for emergency medical assistance if the symptoms don't improve or if the athlete goes into respiratory or cardiac arrest. 3. Monitor breathing and provide CPR if needed. 4. Place an unresponsive athlete in the recovery position (if uninjured) or HAINES position (if injured) to allow fluids or vomit to drain from the mouth. 5. Treat for shock if necessary and send for emergency medical assistance if it occurs. 6. If the athlete recovers quickly, speak to the parents and send the athlete to a physician.

12

Weather-Related Problems

LEARNING OBJECTIVES

In this unit, you will learn

- how to prevent heat-, cold-, and lightning-related injuries and illnesses;
- how to identify the symptoms and signs of heat cramps;
- how to identify and differentiate between the symptoms and signs of heat exhaustion and heatstroke;
- how to identify the symptoms and signs of first-, second-, and third-degree frostbite and mild to severe hypothermia; and
- what first aid care to provide for heat cramps, heat exhaustion, heatstroke, frostbite, hypothermia, and lightning injuries.

WHAT TO READ

Read chapter 11, "Weather-Related Problems," in *Sport First Aid.*

ACTIVITY 12.1

Responding to Weather-Related Problems

Instructions

1. Review each of the scenarios and identify the causes, symptoms, and signs of the illness described in the scenario.

2. For each scenario, complete the following steps, using *Sport First Aid* as a reference:

   a. In the Causes, Symptoms, and Signs table on page 164, find the column that lists information for the illness described in the scenario. Write the illness name and scenario name (e.g., "Scenario 2, Steve") at the top of the appropriate column.

   b. In the First Aid table on page 166, find the column that shows the steps to take for the illness described in the scenario, and write the illness name and scenario name at the top of the appropriate column.

► *Scenario 1, Julia* -

It's a cold, sleeting, blustery day, and your long-distance runners have just returned from their training run. Julia, in particular, can't seem to stop shivering. Julia is normally the cheerleader of the team, but today she's slumped in a chair and barely notices when you approach her. You check her pulse, and it's surprisingly slow. Julia's breathing seems slow as well. You ask Julia how she feels, and she says that she thinks she could lie down on the floor and fall asleep.

▶ Scenario 2, Steve -

It's a postseason game, and your football players are shivering on the sidelines. During halftime, you ask the players to make sure they keep warm—stand by the portable heaters, wear gloves, and so forth. Steve speaks up and tells you it's too late for him. He laughs and tells you he can't feel his ears. Everyone chuckles, but you know to take this more seriously. As the team hustles back on the field, you pull Steve aside and take a closer look. His ears actually look white and waxlike to you. Steve tells you that now, after he has sat in the locker room during halftime, his ears are burning and tingling.

▶ Scenario 3, Hector -

After running a play during a hot preseason practice, Hector pulls up short and grabs his thigh, grimacing in pain. You ask him what's wrong, and he says that he thinks he has a muscle cramp. You touch his quadriceps muscle and can feel muscle spasms. You ask Hector if he's been drinking at each scheduled drink break. He quietly shakes his head no.

▶ Scenario 4, Nancy -

Nancy, one of your soccer players, looks confused. It's a hot, humid day, and you've been offering water breaks every 15 minutes. You know that most of your athletes were susceptible to the heat even before practice started because they spent their afternoon in a hot school building. Now you're keeping an eye on Nancy. She stumbles a little and uncharacteristically snaps at a teammate. You quickly come to Nancy's side and assess her. Her pulse is rapid, and she's breathing fast. Her skin is hot to the touch. You ask Nancy how she feels, and she says that she's hot and just wants to sit down. Before you can react, she collapses on the field, but she is still responsive. You check her pupils, and they look very small.

Causes, Symptoms, and Signs Table

Illness name: _____ Scenario name: _____		Illness name: _____ Scenario name: _____	
Causes • Dehydration • Electrolyte (sodium and potassium) loss • Decreased blood flow to the muscles • Fatigue		**Causes** • Prolonged exposure to a wet, windy, and cold environment • Extreme fatigue, such as that suffered after competition in a marathon or triathlon • Dehydration	
Symptoms • Pain • Fatigue		**Symptoms** When the body temperature drops below 95 degrees: • Irritability • Drowsiness • Lethargy	
Sign • Severe muscle spasms, often in the quadriceps, hamstrings, or calves		**Signs** From 90 to 95 degrees (mild to moderate hypothermia): • Loss of coordination • Loss of sensation • Shivering • Pale and hard skin • Numbness • Irritability • Mild confusion • Depression • Withdrawn • Slow, irregular pulse • Slowed breathing • Sluggish movements • Inability to walk • Difficulty speaking	From 86 to 90 degrees (severe hypothermia): • Hallucinations • Dilated pupils • Decreasing pulse rate • Decreasing breathing rate • Confusion • Semiresponsiveness • Shivering stops • Muscle rigidity • Exposed skin blue and puffy 85 degrees and below (also severe hypothermia): • Unresponsiveness • Respiratory arrest • Erratic to no pulse

Illness name:	Illness name:
_____	_____
Scenario name:	Scenario name:
_____	_____

Cause	Cause
• A malfunction in the brain's temperature control center, caused by severe dehydration, fever, or inadequate balance of the body's temperature regulation	• Exposure of body parts to cold, causing tissues to freeze and blood vessels to constrict

Symptoms	Symptom
• Feels extremely hot • Nausea • Irritability • Fatigue	• Painful, itchy, burning, or tingling areas that may become numb as the frostbite worsens. These symptoms may recur when the affected areas are rewarmed.

Signs	Signs
• Hot and flushed or red skin • Very high body temperature—rectal temperature 104 degrees or more • Rapid pulse • Rapid breathing • Constricted pupils • Vomiting • Diarrhea • Confusion • Possible seizures • Possible unresponsiveness • Possible respiratory or cardiac arrest	First-degree frostbite (superficial): • Red or flushed skin that may turn white or gray Second-degree frostbite: • Firm, white, and waxy skin • Blisters and purple tint to skin may appear when the area is rewarmed Third-degree frostbite (deep): • Blisters • Bluish skin • Frostbitten area feels very cold and stiff

First Aid Table

Illness name:	Illness name:
_____	_____
Scenario name:	Scenario name:
_____	_____
First Aid Mild to moderate hypothermia: 1. Move the athlete to a warm area. 2. Send for emergency medical assistance. 3. Gently remove cold and wet clothes. 4. Wrap the athlete in blankets. 5. Monitor and treat for shock as needed. 6. Give warm fluids, such as hot tea or cider, to a responsive athlete. Severe hypothermia: 1. Send for emergency medical assistance. 2. Cover the athlete with blankets. 3. Handle the athlete very carefully. Excessive movements or jarring may cause cold blood to recirculate to the heart and cause it to stop. 4. Monitor breathing and provide CPR if needed. 5. Monitor and treat for shock as needed.	**First Aid** 1. Send for emergency medical assistance. 2. Immediately remove excess clothing and equipment and immerse athlete in cold water (wading pool or tub). 3. Position the athlete in a semireclining position (if unresponsive, place the athlete in the recovery position (if uninjured) or HAINES position (if injured) to allow fluids and vomit to drain from the mouth). 4. Monitor breathing and provide CPR if needed. 5. Monitor and treat for shock as needed (do not cover the athlete with blankets). 6. Give the athlete cool water or sports beverage to drink (if responsive and able to ingest fluid).

Illness name:	Illness name:
_____	_____
Scenario name:	Scenario name:
_____	_____

First Aid

1. Rest the athlete.
2. Assist the athlete with stretching the affected muscle.
3. Give the athlete a sports beverage (containing sodium) to drink.
4. If the spasms do not stop with stretching or after a few minutes of rest, look for other possible causes.
5. If spasms continue or other injuries are found, inform parents or guardian and send athlete to a physician.

First Aid

First- and second-degree frostbite:

1. Move the athlete to a warm area.
2. Remove wet and cold clothing.
3. Monitor and treat for shock as needed and call for emergency medical assistance if it occurs.
4. Rewarm the area by soaking it in clean, warm water (100 to 105 degrees Fahrenheit).
5. Call the athlete's parents or guardian to take the athlete to a physician.

Third-degree frostbite:

1. Send for emergency medical assistance.
2. Move the athlete to a warm area.
3. Remove wet and cold clothing.
4. Monitor breathing and provide CPR if needed.
5. Monitor and treat for shock as needed.

ACTIVITY 12.1

Responding to Weather-Related Problems

Causes, Symptoms, and Signs Table

Illness name: *Heat cramps*	Illness name: *Hypothermia*	
Scenario name: *Scenario 3, Hector*	Scenario name: *Scenario 1, Julia*	
Causes • Dehydration • Electrolyte (sodium and potassium) loss • Decreased blood flow to the muscles • Fatigue	**Causes** • Prolonged exposure to a wet, windy, and cold environment • Extreme fatigue, such as that suffered after competition in a marathon or triathlon • Dehydration	
Symptoms • Pain • Fatigue	**Symptoms** When the body temperature drops below 95 degrees: • Irritability • Drowsiness • Lethargy	
Sign • Severe muscle spasms, often in the quadriceps, hamstrings, or calves	**Signs** From 90 to 95 degrees (mild to moderate hypothermia): • Loss of coordination • Loss of sensation • Shivering • Pale and hard skin • Numbness • Irritability • Mild confusion • Depression • Withdrawn • Slow, irregular pulse • Slowed breathing • Sluggish movements • Inability to walk • Difficulty speaking	From 86 to 90 degrees (severe hypothermia): • Hallucinations • Dilated pupils • Decreasing pulse rate • Decreasing breathing rate • Confusion • Semiresponsiveness • Shivering stops • Muscle rigidity • Exposed skin blue and puffy 85 degrees and below (also severe hypothermia): • Unresponsiveness • Respiratory arrest • Erratic to no pulse

Illness name: _Heatstroke_	Illness name: _Frostbite, second degree_
Scenario name: _Scenario 4, Nancy_	Scenario name: _Scenario 2, Steve_
Cause • A malfunction in the brain's temperature control center, caused by severe dehydration, fever, or inadequate balance of the body's temperature regulation	**Cause** • Exposure of body parts to cold, causing tissues to freeze and blood vessels to constrict
Symptoms • Feels extremely hot • Nausea • Irritability • Fatigue	**Symptom** • Painful, itchy, burning, or tingling areas that may become numb as the frostbite worsens. These symptoms may recur when the affected areas are rewarmed.
Signs • Hot and flushed or red skin • Very high body temperature—rectal temperature 104 degrees or more • Rapid pulse • Rapid breathing • Constricted pupils • Vomiting • Diarrhea • Confusion • Possible seizures • Unresponsiveness • Possible respiratory or cardiac arrest	**Signs** First-degree frostbite (superficial): • Red or flushed skin that may turn white or gray Second-degree frostbite: • Firm, white, and waxy skin • Blisters and purple tint to skin may appear when the area is rewarmed Third-degree frostbite (deep): • Blisters • Bluish skin • Frostbitten area feels very cold and stiff

First Aid Table

Illness name: _Hypothermia_ Scenario name: _Scenario 1, Julia_	Illness name: _Heatstroke_ Scenario name: _Scenario 4, Nancy_
First Aid Mild to moderate hypothermia: 1. Move the athlete to a warm area. 2. Send for emergency medical assistance. 3. Gently remove cold and wet clothes. 4. Wrap the athlete in blankets. 5. Monitor and treat for shock as needed. 6. Give warm fluids, such as hot tea or cider, to a responsive athlete. Severe hypothermia: 1. Send for emergency medical assistance. 2. Cover the athlete with blankets. 3. Handle the athlete very carefully. Excessive movements or jarring may cause cold blood to recirculate to the heart and cause it to stop. 4. Monitor breathing and provide CPR if needed. 5. Monitor and treat for shock as needed.	**First Aid** 1. Send for emergency medical assistance. 2. Immediately remove excess clothing and equipment and immerse athlete in cold water (wading pool or tub). 3. Position the athlete in a semireclining position (if unresponsive, place the athlete in the recovery position (if uninjured) or HAINES position (if injured) to allow fluids and vomit to drain from the mouth). 4. Monitor breathing and provide CPR if needed. 5. Monitor and treat for shock as needed (do not cover the athlete with blankets). 6. Give the athlete cool water or sports beverage to drink (if responsive and able to ingest fluid).

Illness name: _Heat cramps_	Illness name: _Frostbite, second degree_
Scenario name: _Scenario 3, Hector_	Scenario name: _Scenario 2, Steve_
First Aid 1. Rest the athlete. 2. Assist the athlete with stretching the affected muscle. 3. Give the athlete a sports beverage (containing sodium) to drink. 4. If the spasms do not stop with stretching or after a few minutes of rest, look for other possible causes. 5. If spasms continue or other injuries are found, inform parents or guardian and send athlete to a physician.	**First Aid** First- and second-degree frostbite: 1. Move the athlete to a warm area. 2. Remove wet and cold clothing. 3. Monitor and treat for shock as needed and call for emergency medical assistance if it occurs. 4. Rewarm the area by soaking it in clean, warm water (100 to 105 degrees Fahrenheit). 5. Call the athlete's parents or guardian to take the athlete to a physician. Third-degree frostbite: 1. Send for emergency medical assistance. 2. Move the athlete to a warm area. 3. Remove wet and cold clothing. 4. Monitor breathing and provide CPR if needed. 5. Monitor and treat for shock as needed.

Upper Body Musculoskeletal Injuries

LEARNING OBJECTIVES

In this unit, you will learn

- how to recognize upper body musculoskeletal injuries,
- what first aid care to provide for each of these types of injuries,
- how to prevent upper body musculoskeletal injuries, and
- what conditions are required before an injured athlete can return to play.

WHAT TO READ

Read chapter 12, "Upper Body Musculoskeletal Injuries," in *Sport First Aid.*

ACTIVITY 13.1

Responding to Upper Body Musculoskeletal Injuries

Instructions

1. Review each of the scenarios and identify the causes, symptoms, and signs of the injury described in the scenario.

2. For each scenario, complete the following steps, using *Sport First Aid* as a reference:

   a. In the Causes, Symptoms, and Signs table on page 176, find the column that lists information for the injury described in the scenario. Write the injury name and scenario name (e.g., "Scenario 2, Gretchen") at the top of the appropriate column.

   b. In the First Aid table on page 178, find the column that shows the steps to take for the injury described in the scenario, and write the injury name and scenario name at the top of the appropriate column.

▶ **Scenario 1, Dave** -

There is a little jostling in the locker room one night, and Dave accidentally shuts his locker on his fingers. He yelps in pain, and you come over to see what happened. Dave's index finger is swelling quickly. Dave tries to bend his finger, but it's too painful to do so. You tap the end of the finger, and Dave winces.

▶ **Scenario 2, Gretchen** -

Gretchen overrotates in her dismount from the uneven bars and falls forward onto her outstretched hand. She stands and completes her performance, but you can tell she is in pain as she walks off the platform. You ask Gretchen to try bending her wrist, and she finds it very painful to do so. She can hardly rotate her palm up and down without crying out. Her wrist is swelling, and the palm side of her wrist is tender to the touch.

▶ Scenario 3, Jackson -

Jackson fell hard to the court after getting tangled up defending the basket. He tried to break his fall with his left hand and arm. You can immediately tell that Jackson is in a great deal of pain. His arm is swelling, and even gently touching the outside of his forearm causes pain in this tough player. You ask Jackson how much he can move his arm, and he cannot twist his forearm to turn his palm up or down. You see a slight deformity toward the end of his forearm.

▶ Scenario 4, Bryan -

While battling another player for control of the soccer ball, Bryan gets hit hard in the elbow by the opponent's elbow. He rubs his elbow for a minute and then continues to play. After a few minutes, you can tell something is still wrong. You call him to the sidelines to check things out. You don't see any obvious deformity. You ask Bryan exactly where he got hit, and he points to the inside back of his elbow. Bryan tells you that pain is shooting from his elbow down his arm, toward his hand. You compare the grip strength in both of Bryan's hands, and you find the hand on his injured side to have much less strength than the other. You gently touch the point of impact, and Bryan cringes in pain.

▶ Scenario 5, Jessica -

During a basketball game, Jessica has her arms raised to her side to guard against a pass when her upper arm gets pulled back hard by another player who is trying to go around her. Jessica immediately grabs her shoulder in pain. She tells you she heard a pop in her shoulder and now her arm feels loose. You notice that Jessica is holding her arm slightly out to her side. You ask her if she can move her arm, and she is unable to do so. When you visually compare the two shoulders, Jessica's right shoulder looks flat instead of rounded.

▶ Scenario 6, Raul -

Raul, one of your wide receivers, stretches to catch a pass but misses and falls on his shoulder. Raul walks to the sidelines holding his shoulder. He's obviously in a great deal of pain. He explains how he fell, and when you ask where it hurts, he points to the outer edge of his clavicle. You can see and feel a slight bump at the outside end of the clavicle. You ask him to try moving his arm in different directions. Raul can reach his arm across his body and raise it overhead, but his movements are tentative because of the extreme pain. Raul has little trouble shrugging his shoulders.

Causes, Symptoms, and Signs Table

Injury name: _____ Scenario name: _____	Injury name: _____ Scenario name: _____	Injury name: _____ Scenario name: _____
Cause • Direct blow to the inside back of the elbow	**Causes** • Direct blow to the end of the finger or thumb • Forceful crushing or pinching of finger or thumb between two objects	**Causes** • Direct blow • Falling on an outstretched hand
Symptoms Mild: • Tingling down the forearm and hand (if injury bruises nerve) that lasts a few minutes • Mild pain shooting from elbow down to forearm Moderate to severe: • Tingling down the forearm and hand (if injury bruises nerve) that lasts more than five minutes • Moderate to severe pain shooting from elbow down to forearm	**Symptoms** • Pain with bending or straightening the finger or thumb • Pain when the end of the finger is tapped	**Symptom** • Pain
Signs Mild: • Mild point tenderness Moderate to severe: • Moderate to severe point tenderness • Loss of grip strength • Swelling • Discoloration • Hand weakness • Loss of sensation in ring and little fingers	**Signs** • Swelling • Deformity • Inability to bend or straighten finger	**Signs** • Swelling • Deformity • Severe point tenderness • Inability to rotate or twist forearm to turn palm up or down • Inability to bend or straighten wrist or elbow (depending on the site of the injury along the forearm) • Bluish skin on hand or fingers (if fracture, injures blood vessels) • Loss of sensation and tingling in hand and fingers (if fracture injures nerves)

Injury name:	Injury name:	Injury name:
Scenario name:	Scenario name:	Scenario name:
Causes • Direct blow to the top or side of the shoulder • Fall on outstretched arm	**Causes** • Backward blow to upper arm while it is raised to the side • Forceful contraction of the shoulder muscles • Fall on outstretched arm	**Causes** • Torsion (twisting) injury • Falling on an outstretched hand
Symptoms Grade I: • Mild pain along the outer edge of the clavicle (collarbone) • Mild pain with raising the arm overhead • Mild pain with reaching the arm across the body Grades II and III: • Moderate to severe pain along the outer edge of the clavicle (collarbone) • Moderate to severe pain with raising the arm overhead • Moderate to severe pain with reaching the arm across the body	**Symptoms** • Intense pain where the upper arm bone connects to the shoulder blade • Sense of looseness or giving away • Tingling in arm or hand (caused by the displaced bone pinching nerves) • Felt or heard a pop	**Symptoms** Grade I: • Mild pain along sides, back, or front of wrist • Mild pain with bending wrist to extremes • Mild pain with rotating palm up or down Grades II and III: • Moderate to severe pain along sides, back, or front of wrist • Moderate to severe pain with bending wrist to extremes • Moderate to severe pain with rotating palm up or down • Wrist feels loose or unstable
Signs Grade I: • Slight elevation of the end of the clavicle • Mild point tenderness over outer edge of the collarbone Grades II and III: • Moderate to severe elevation of the outer edge of the clavicle • Moderate to severe point tenderness over outer edge of the collarbone	**Signs** • Inability to move the arm • Shoulder appears flat instead of rounded • Arm is held slightly out to the side of the body • Lack of sensation in the arm or hand (caused by the displaced bone pinching nerves and arteries) • Bluish arm or hand (caused by the displaced bone disrupting blood supply)	**Signs** Grade I: • Mild point tenderness over the sides, back, or front of wrist Grades II and III: • Moderate to severe point tenderness over the sides, back, or front of wrist • Decreased grip strength • Swelling • Deformity if sprain results in wrist bone shifting out of position

First Aid Table

Injury name:	Injury name:	Injury name:
Scenario name:	Scenario name:	Scenario name:
First Aid Grade I: 1. Rest the athlete from painful activities. 2. Apply ice. 3. Refer the athlete to a physician if symptoms and signs worsen (occur more often, especially with daily activities) or do not subside within a few days. Grades II and III: 1. Rest the arm from all activities. 2. Splint the wrist and hand and secure to the body with a sling. 3. Monitor and treat for shock if needed and send for emergency medical assistance if it occurs. 4. Apply ice and send the athlete to a physician.	**First Aid** 1. Send for emergency medical assistance. 2. If emergency medical assistance is delayed more than 20 minutes, stabilize the arm in the position in which you found it. 3. Do not try to put the humerus back into the socket. 4. Monitor and treat for shock as needed. 5. Apply ice.	**First Aid** Mild: 1. Rest the athlete from activity until numbness and tingling are gone, and until the athlete has full elbow range of motion and full hand strength. Moderate to severe: 1. Rest the athlete from all activity. 2. Immobilize the arm with a sling, if tolerated. 3. Treat for shock as needed and send for emergency medical assistance if it occurs. 4. Send the athlete to a physician.

First Aid Table

Injury name: _____ Scenario name: _____	Injury name: _____ Scenario name: _____	Injury name: _____ Scenario name: _____
First Aid Send for emergency medical assistance if bones are grossly displaced or sticking through the skin, if there are signs of nerve damage or disrupted circulation, or if the athlete is suffering from shock. If none of the above, do the following: 1. Splint the arm in the position in which you found it. 2. Monitor and treat for shock as needed and send for emergency medical assistance if it occurs. 3. Apply ice (avoid the nerve that runs to the hand) and send the athlete to a physician.	**First Aid** Grade I: 1. Rest the athlete from painful activities. 2. Apply ice. 3. Refer the athlete to a physician if symptoms and signs worsen (occur more often, especially with daily activities) or do not subside within a few days. Grades II and III: 1. Immobilize the arm with a sling and secure the arm to the body with an elastic wrap. 2. Monitor and treat for shock as needed and send for emergency medical assistance if it occurs. 3. Apply ice and send the athlete to a physician (if shock does not occur).	**First Aid** Send for emergency medical assistance if bones are sticking through the skin, if there are signs of nerve damage or disrupted circulation, or if the athlete is suffering from shock. If none of the above, do the following: 1. Immobilize the hand and fingers. 2. Secure the hand to the body by applying an arm sling. 3. Monitor and treat for shock as needed and send for emergency medical assistance if it occurs. 4. Apply ice and send the athlete to a physician. * Although mentioned in the textbook, grossly displaced finger bones do not need emergency medical personnel.

ACTIVITY 13.1
Responding to Upper Body Musculoskeletal Injuries

Causes, Symptoms, and Signs Table

Injury name: Ulnar nerve contusion Scenario name: Scenario 4, Bryan	Injury name: Finger fracture Scenario name: Scenario 1, Dave	Injury name: Forearm fracture Scenario name: Scenario 3, Jackson
Cause • Direct blow to the inside back of the elbow	**Causes** • Direct blow to the end of the finger or thumb • Forceful crushing or pinching of finger or thumb between two objects	**Causes** • Direct blow • Falling on an outstretched hand
Symptoms Mild: • Tingling down the forearm and hand (if injury bruises nerve) that lasts a few minutes • Mild pain shooting from elbow down to forearm Moderate to severe: • Tingling down the forearm and hand (if injury bruises nerve) that lasts more than five minutes • Moderate to severe pain shooting from elbow down to forearm	**Symptoms** • Pain with bending or straightening the finger or thumb • Pain when the end of the finger is tapped	**Symptom** • Pain
Signs Mild: • Mild point tenderness Moderate to severe: • Moderate to severe point tenderness • Loss of grip strength • Swelling • Discoloration • Hand weakness • Loss of sensation in ring and little fingers	**Signs** • Swelling • Deformity • Inability to bend or straighten finger	**Signs** • Swelling • Deformity • Severe point tenderness • Inability to rotate or twist forearm to turn palm up or down • Inability to bend or straighten wrist or elbow (depending on the site of the injury along the forearm) • Bluish skin on hand or fingers (if fracture, injures blood vessels) • Loss of sensation and tingling in hand and fingers (if fracture injures nerves)

Injury name: *AC joint sprain,* *Grade II or III* Scenario name: *Scenario 6, Raul*	Injury name: *Shoulder dislocation* Scenario name: *Scenario 5, Jessica*	Injury name: *Wrist sprain, Grade II* Scenario name: *Scenario 2, Gretchen*
Causes • Direct blow to the top or side of the shoulder • Fall on outstretched arm	**Causes** • Backward blow to upper arm while it is raised to the side • Forceful contraction of the shoulder muscles • Fall on outstretched arm	**Causes** • Torsion (twisting) injury • Falling on an outstretched hand
Symptoms Grade I: • Mild pain along the outer edge of the clavicle (collarbone) • Mild pain with raising the arm overhead • Mild pain with reaching the arm across the body Grades II and III: • Moderate to severe pain along the outer edge of the clavicle (collarbone) • Moderate to severe pain with raising the arm overhead • Moderate to severe pain with reaching the arm across the body	**Symptoms** • Intense pain where the upper arm bone connects to the shoulder blade • Sense of looseness or giving away • Tingling in arm or hand (caused by the displaced bone pinching nerves) • Felt or heard a pop	**Symptoms** Grade I: • Mild pain along sides, back, or front of wrist • Mild pain with bending wrist to extremes • Mild pain with rotating palm up or down Grades II and III: • Moderate to severe pain along sides, back, or front of wrist • Moderate to severe pain with bending wrist to extremes • Moderate to severe pain with rotating palm up or down • Wrist feels loose or unstable
Signs Grade I: • Slight elevation of the end of the clavicle • Mild point tenderness over outer edge of the collarbone Grades II and III: • Moderate to severe elevation of the outer edge of the clavicle • Moderate to severe point tenderness over outer edge of the collarbone	**Signs** • Inability to move the arm • Shoulder appears flat instead of rounded • Arm is held slightly out to the side of the body • Lack of sensation in the arm or hand (caused by the displaced bone pinching nerves and arteries) • Bluish arm or hand (caused by the displaced bone disrupting blood supply)	**Signs** Grade I: • Mild point tenderness over the sides, back, or front of wrist Grades II and III: • Moderate to severe point tenderness over the sides, back, or front of wrist • Decreased grip strength • Swelling • Deformity if sprain results in wrist bone shifting out of position

First Aid Table

Injury name: _Wrist sprain, Grade II_	Injury name: _Shoulder dislocation_	Injury name: _Ulnar nerve contusion_
Scenario name: _Scenario 2, Gretchen_	Scenario name: _Scenario 5, Jessica_	Scenario name: _Scenario 4, Bryan_
First Aid Grade I: 1. Rest the athlete from painful activities. 2. Apply ice. 3. Refer the athlete to a physician if symptoms and signs worsen (occur more often, especially with daily activities) or do not subside within a few days. Grades II and III: 1. Rest the arm from all activities. 2. Splint the wrist and hand and secure to the body with a sling. 3. Monitor and treat for shock if needed and send for emergency medical assistance if it occurs. 4. Apply ice and send the athlete to a physician.	**First Aid** 1. Send for emergency medical assistance. 2. If emergency medical assistance is delayed more than 20 minutes, stabilize the arm in the position in which you found it. 3. Do not try to put the humerus back into the socket. 4. Monitor and treat for shock as needed. 5. Apply ice.	**First Aid** Mild: 1. Rest the athlete from activity until numbness and tingling are gone, and until the athlete has full elbow range of motion and full hand strength. Moderate to severe: 1. Rest the athlete from all activity. 2. Immobilize the arm with a sling, if tolerated. 3. Treat for shock as needed and send for emergency medical assistance if it occurs. 4. Send the athlete to a physician.

First Aid Table

Injury name:	Injury name:	Injury name:
Forearm fracture	*AC joint sprain, Grade II or III*	*Finger fracture*
Scenario name:	**Scenario name:**	**Scenario name:**
Scenario 3, Jackson	*Scenario 6, Raul*	*Scenario 1, Dave*
First Aid Send for emergency medical assistance if bones are grossly displaced or sticking through the skin, if there are signs of nerve damage or disrupted circulation, or if the athlete is suffering from shock. If none of the above, do the following: 1. Splint the arm in the position in which you found it. 2. Monitor and treat for shock as needed and send for emergency medical assistance if it occurs. 3. Apply ice (avoid the nerve that runs to the hand) and send the athlete to a physician.	**First Aid** Grade I: 1. Rest the athlete from painful activities. 2. Apply ice. 3. Refer the athlete to a physician if symptoms and signs worsen (occur more often, especially with daily activities) or do not subside within a few days. Grades II and III: 1. Immobilize the arm with a sling and secure the arm to the body with an elastic wrap. 2. Monitor and treat for shock as needed and send for emergency medical assistance if it occurs. 3. Apply ice and send the athlete to a physician (if shock does not occur).	**First Aid** Send for emergency medical assistance if bones are sticking through the skin, if there are signs of nerve damage or disrupted circulation, or if the athlete is suffering from shock. If none of the above, do the following: 1. Immobilize the hand and fingers. 2. Secure the hand to the body by applying an arm sling. 3. Monitor and treat for shock as needed and send for emergency medical assistance if it occurs. 4. Apply ice and send the athlete to a physician. * Although mentioned in the textbook, grossly displaced finger bones do not need emergency medical personnel.

Lower Body Musculoskeletal Injuries

LEARNING OBJECTIVES

In this unit, you will learn

- how to recognize lower body musculoskeletal injuries,
- what first aid care to provide for each of these types of injuries,
- how to prevent lower body musculoskeletal injuries, and
- what conditions are required before an injured athlete can return to play.

WHAT TO READ

Read chapter 13, "Lower Body Musculoskeletal Injuries," in *Sport First Aid.*

ACTIVITY 14.1

Responding to Lower Body Musculoskeletal Injuries

Instructions

1. Review each of the scenarios and identify the causes, symptoms, and signs of the injury described in the scenario.

2. For each scenario, complete the following steps, using *Sport First Aid* as a reference:

    a. In the Causes, Symptoms, and Signs table on page 188, find the column that lists information for the injury described in the scenario. Write the injury name and scenario name (e.g., "Scenario 2, Bryce") at the top of the appropriate column.

    b. In the First Aid table on page 190, find the column that shows the steps to take for the injury described in the scenario, and write the injury name and scenario name at the top of the appropriate column.

▶ *Scenario I, Jeremy* -

Jeremy, one of your basketball players, complains that his lower leg really hurts. You know that Jeremy loves to run and puts in a couple miles a day outside of your practice sessions. You ask him to show you where it hurts, and he points to an area just outside of the tibia. You gently touch the area, and Jeremy says it hurts, but just a little. You ask how long it has been painful. Jeremy tells you that it's been coming on for several weeks. At first it only hurt after his training runs, but now his leg hurts throughout the runs and especially during basketball practice, when he's running and jumping. Jeremy's basketball shoes are in good condition. You ask to see his running shoes, and it's obvious that they're worn out: The soles are cracking, and any arch support they once had is long gone.

▶ Scenario 2, Bryce

Bryce, one of your running backs, tries to free himself from a leg tackle when another defender barrels into him. Bryce falls to the ground, twisting his leg in the process. Bryce doesn't get up, so you quickly run onto the field. Bryce's breathing and circulation are normal, but he's clearly in a lot of pain. He tells you that he heard a snap in his leg. It hurts him to move his leg in any way. His thigh muscles are in spasms, and his leg is turned awkwardly outward.

▶ Scenario 3, Yolanda

During basketball practice, Yolanda clearly isn't performing up to par. You ask her what is wrong, and she complains that her knee hurts. You ask her if it hurts all the time, and she says that it only hurts when she's running or jumping. You prod a little further and learn that Yolanda's knee feels achy after she's been sitting in class for a long time. As you examine Yolanda further, you find that the pain is localized behind the kneecap. Yolanda says it hurts "inside her knee" when you touch her patella.

▶ Scenario 4, Samantha -

Samantha races to catch a fly ball that is just out of her reach. She stretches as far as she can and makes the game-saving catch. After the game, though, Samantha complains that her back hurts. She has mild pain when bending and twisting, and when you touch either side of her low back, Samantha tells you it hurts, though not too much.

▶ Scenario 5, Danielle -

Danielle is dribbling confidently in a soccer game when she trips on a bump in the ground and falls forward, onto her bent knee. She quickly stands and then catches herself with her uninjured leg and drops to the ground. You jog to her and ask her not to move. She's clearly in extreme pain, and she tells you that she heard and felt a pop in her hip. You don't see any deformity. Danielle can move her thigh but says that the hip feels loose. She wants to walk to the sidelines, but you know better.

Causes, Symptoms, and Signs Table

Injury name:	Injury name:	Injury name:
Scenario name:	Scenario name:	Scenario name:

Causes	**Cause**	**Causes**
• Forceful contraction or stretch (tension injury) of shin muscles • Suddenly increasing the intensity of sport or conditioning program • Repeatedly running on an uneven or unyielding surface • Tight calf muscles • Tight Achilles tendon • Weak or inflexible shin muscles • Faulty foot mechanics that fail to absorb shock and allow shock to be transmitted up the lower leg bone • Shoes with inadequate arch support • Worn-out athletic shoes	• 70 to 80 percent of all hip dislocations are caused by the head of the femur (thighbone) dislocating backward out of the socket. Typically, these occur when an athlete lands on a bent knee while the thigh is rotated inward and positioned close to the midline of the body. An example is a running football player who is tackled and falls forward on a bent knee.	• Sudden stretch or contraction of the low back muscles • Weak abdominal muscles • Tight low back muscles and hip muscles

Symptoms	**Symptoms**	**Symptoms**
Grade I: • Mild pain just to the inside or outside of the tibia • Mild pain with running and jumping activities • Pain decreases with rest Grades II and III: • Moderate to severe pain just to the inside or outside of the tibia • Pain with walking • Pain at rest • Moderate to severe pain with running and jumping activities	• Severe pain in hip and thigh • Tingling in leg and foot (if displaced bone pinches nerves) • Sense of looseness or instability • Felt or heard a pop • Knee, lower leg, or even back pain	Grade I: • Mild pain when low back muscles contracted • Mild pain with rising from lying down to sitting • Mild pain when bending forward • Mild pain when arching back • Mild pain when twisting at the waist Grades II and III: • Moderate to severe pain when low back muscles contracted • Moderate to severe pain with rising from lying down to sitting • Moderate to severe pain when bending forward • Moderate to severe pain when arching back • Moderate to severe pain when twisting at the waist

Signs	**Signs**	**Signs**
Grade I: • Slight point tenderness over the site of the injury Grades II and III: • Moderate to severe point tenderness over the site of the injury • Swelling • Decreased ability or inability to run or jump	Subluxation: • Lack of sensation in the leg, foot, or toes (if displaced bone pinches nerves) • Bluish leg, foot, or toes (if displaced bone disrupts blood supply) • Limping	Grade I: • Mild tenderness over site of injury (toward either side from the spine) Grades II and III: • Moderate to severe tenderness over site of injury (toward either side from the spine) • Lump or indentation where the muscle is torn • Back weakness • Bruising (appears a day or two after initial injury)

Injury name: ——————————— Scenario name: ———————————	Injury name: ——————————— Scenario name: ———————————
Causes • Direct blow • Twisting or torsion injury	**Causes** • Direct blow to the top of the patella • Inability of the patella to properly track in the groove in the femur • Repeated episodes of patellar dislocation and subluxation • Weak quadriceps and gluteal (buttocks) muscles or inflexible quadriceps, hamstring, and calf muscles • Previous blow to the patella
Symptoms • Heard or felt a pop or snap • Grating feeling • Pain at the site of the injury when gently squeezing the thigh above and then below the injury • Severe pain with any movement	**Symptoms** Mild: • Mild pain with running, jumping, or using stairs • Mild pain behind the patella • Grating feeling behind the patella • Mild achiness while sitting for extended periods Moderate to severe: • Moderate to severe pain with running, jumping, or using stairs • Moderate to severe pain behind the patella • Grating feeling behind the patella • Moderate to severe achiness while sitting for extended periods
Signs • Deformity • Inability to move thigh • Lack of sensation in the leg, foot, or toes (if displaced bone pinches nerves) • Bluish leg, foot, or toes (if displaced bone disrupts blood supply) • Muscle spasm	**Signs** Mild: • Mild point tenderness underneath the patella Moderate to severe: • Moderate to severe point tenderness underneath the patella • Decreased ability or inability to forcefully straighten the knee, especially when jumping, lifting weights, and running • Limping

First Aid Table

Injury name: _____ Scenario name: _____	Injury name: _____ Scenario name: _____	Injury name: _____ Scenario name: _____

First Aid
Mild:
1. Rest the athlete from painful activities.
2. Apply ice.
3. Refer the athlete to a physician if symptoms and signs worsen (occur more often, especially with daily activities) or do not subside within a few days.
 	
Moderate to severe:
1. Rest the athlete from all activities.
2. Monitor and treat for shock as needed and send for emergency medical assistance if it occurs.
3. Prevent the athlete from walking on the injured leg.
4. Apply ice to the injury and send the athlete to a physician (if shock does not occur).
	First Aid
	1. Send for emergency medical assistance.
	2. Prevent the athlete from moving the hip and the entire leg.
	3. Monitor and treat for shock as needed.
	4. Apply ice for 15 minutes.
		First Aid
		Grade I:
		1. Rest the athlete from all activities causing pain.
		2. Apply ice.
		3. Refer the athlete to a physician if symptoms and signs worsen (occur more often, especially with daily activities) or do not subside within a few days.
		
		Grades II and III:
		1. Rest the athlete from all activities.
		2. Monitor and treat for shock as needed and send for emergency medical assistance if it occurs.
		3. Send for emergency medical assistance if any of the following are present:
		  a. Signs of fracture—obvious deformity, or pain at the site of the injury when compressing the tibia or fibula above, then below the site of the injury
		  b. Symptoms and signs of compression to nerves (tingling or numbness in foot or toes)
		  c. Symptoms and signs of disrupted blood supply (bluish foot or toes that are cold to the touch)
		4. Prevent the athlete from walking on the injured foot.
		5. Apply ice to the injury and send the athlete to a physician (if emergency medical assistance is not sent for).

First Aid Table

Injury name:	Injury name:
_____	_____
Scenario name:	**Scenario name:**
_____	_____
First Aid	**First Aid**
Subluxation:	Grade I:

1. Prevent the athlete from walking on the injured leg.
2. Monitor and treat for shock as needed and send for emergency medical assistance if it occurs.
3. Send for emergency medical assistance if the athlete has extreme pain, limited hip motion, or signs and symptoms of nerve damage or disrupted blood supply.
4. Apply ice to the injury and send the athlete to a physician.
	1. Rest the athlete from painful activities.
	2. Apply ice.
	3. Refer the athlete to a physician if symptoms and signs worsen (occur more often, especially with daily activities) or do not subside within a few days.
	
	Grades II and III:
	1. Rest the athlete from all activities.
	2. Monitor and treat for shock as needed and send for emergency medical assistance if it occurs.
	3. Send for emergency medical assistance if
	  a. the injury was caused by a direct blow and resulted in spine deformity or tenderness directly over the spine, or
	  b. the athlete has signs and symptoms of nerve damage— sharp shooting pain, numbness or tingling down one leg, leg weakness, lower extremity paralysis, or incontinence.
	4. Apply ice to the injury and send the athlete to a physician (if emergency medical assistance is not sent for).

ACTIVITY 14.1 — Responding to Lower Body Musculoskeletal Injuries

Causes, Symptoms, and Signs Table

Injury name:	Injury name:	Injury name:
Shin splints	_Hip subluxation_	_Low back strain, Grade I_
Scenario name:	**Scenario name:**	**Scenario name:**
Scenario 1, Jeremy	_Scenario 5, Danielle_	_Scenario 4, Samantha_
Causes • Forceful contraction or stretch (tension injury) of shin muscles • Suddenly increasing the intensity of sport or conditioning program • Repeatedly running on an uneven or unyielding surface • Tight calf muscles • Tight Achilles tendon • Weak or inflexible shin muscles • Faulty foot mechanics that fail to absorb shock and allow shock to be transmitted up the lower leg bone • Shoes with inadequate arch support • Worn-out athletic shoes	**Cause** • 70 to 80 percent of all hip dislocations are caused by the head of the femur (thighbone) dislocating backward out of the socket. Typically, these occur when an athlete lands on a bent knee while the thigh is rotated inward and positioned close to the midline of the body. An example is a running football player who is tackled and falls forward on a bent knee.	**Causes** • Sudden stretch or contraction of the low back muscles • Weak abdominal muscles • Tight low back muscles and hip muscles
Symptoms Grade I: • Mild pain just to the inside or outside of the tibia • Mild pain with running and jumping activities • Pain decreases with rest Grades II and III: • Moderate to severe pain just to the inside or outside of the tibia • Pain with walking • Pain at rest • Moderate to severe pain with running and jumping activities	**Symptoms** • Severe pain in hip and thigh • Tingling in leg and foot (if displaced bone pinches nerves) • Sense of looseness or instability • Felt or heard a pop • Knee, lower leg, or even back pain	**Symptoms** Grade I: • Mild pain when low back muscles contracted • Mild pain with rising from lying down to sitting • Mild pain when bending forward • Mild pain when arching back • Mild pain when twisting at the waist Grades II and III: • Moderate to severe pain when low back muscles contracted • Moderate to severe pain with rising from lying down to sitting • Moderate to severe pain when bending forward • Moderate to severe pain when arching back • Moderate to severe pain when twisting at the waist
Signs Grade I: • Slight point tenderness over the site of the injury Grades II and III: • Moderate to severe point tenderness over the site of the injury • Swelling • Decreased ability or inability to run or jump	**Signs** Subluxation: • Lack of sensation in the leg, foot, or toes (if displaced bone pinches nerves) • Bluish leg, foot, or toes (if displaced bone disrupts blood supply) • Limping	**Signs** Grade I: • Mild tenderness over site of injury (toward either side from the spine) Grades II and III: • Moderate to severe tenderness over site of injury (toward either side from the spine) • Lump or indentation where the muscle is torn • Back weakness • Bruising (appears a day or two after initial injury)

Injury name:	Injury name:
Thigh fracture	*Anterior knee pain*
Scenario name:	**Scenario name:**
Scenario 2, Bryce	*Scenario 3, Yolanda*
Causes • Direct blow • Twisting or torsion injury	**Causes** • Direct blow to the top of the patella • Inability of the patella to properly track in the groove in the femur • Repeated episodes of patellar dislocation and subluxation • Weak quadriceps and gluteal (buttocks) muscles or inflexible quadriceps, hamstring, and calf muscles • Previous blow to the patella
Symptoms • Heard or felt a pop or snap • Grating feeling • Pain at the site of the injury when gently squeezing the thigh above and then below the injury • Severe pain with any movement	**Symptoms** Mild: • Mild pain with running, jumping, or using stairs • Mild pain behind the patella • Grating feeling behind the patella • Mild achiness while sitting for extended periods Moderate to severe: • Moderate to severe pain with running, jumping, or using stairs • Moderate to severe pain behind the patella • Grating feeling behind the patella • Moderate to severe achiness while sitting for extended periods
Signs • Deformity • Inability to move thigh • Lack of sensation in the leg, foot, or toes (if displaced bone pinches nerves) • Bluish leg, foot, or toes (if displaced bone disrupts blood supply) • Muscle spasm	**Signs** Mild: • Mild point tenderness underneath the patella Moderate to severe: • Moderate to severe point tenderness underneath the patella • Decreased ability or inability to forcefully straighten the knee, especially when jumping, lifting weights, and running • Limping

First Aid Table

Injury name: _Anterior knee pain_	Injury name: _Thigh fracture_	Injury name: _Shin splints_
Scenario name: _Scenario 3, Yolanda_	Scenario name: _Scenario 2, Bryce_	Scenario name: _Scenario 1, Jeremy_

First Aid
Mild:
1. Rest the athlete from painful activities.
2. Apply ice.
3. Refer the athlete to a physician if symptoms and signs worsen (occur more often, especially with daily activities) or do not subside within a few days.
 	
Moderate to severe:
1. Rest the athlete from all activities.
2. Monitor and treat for shock as needed and send for emergency medical assistance if it occurs.
3. Prevent the athlete from walking on the injured leg.
4. Apply ice to the injury and send the athlete to a physician (if shock does not occur).
	First Aid
	1. Send for emergency medical assistance.
	2. Prevent the athlete from moving the hip and the entire leg.
	3. Monitor and treat for shock as needed.
	4. Apply ice for 15 minutes.
		First Aid
		Grade I:
		1. Rest the athlete from all activities causing pain.
		2. Apply ice.
		3. Refer the athlete to a physician if symptoms and signs worsen (occur more often, especially with daily activities) or do not subside within a few days.
		
		Grades II and III:
		1. Rest the athlete from all activities.
		2. Monitor and treat for shock as needed and send for emergency medical assistance if it occurs.
		3. Send for emergency medical assistance if any of the following are present:
		  a. Signs of fracture—obvious deformity, or pain at the site of the injury when compressing the tibia or fibula above, then below the site of the injury
		  b. Symptoms and signs of compression to nerves (tingling or numbness in foot or toes)
		  c. Symptoms and signs of disrupted blood supply (bluish foot or toes that are cold to the touch)
		4. Prevent the athlete from walking on the injured foot.
		5. Apply ice to the injury and send the athlete to a physician (if emergency medical assistance is not sent for).

Injury name:	Injury name:
Hip subluxation	*Low back strain, Grade I*
Scenario name:	**Scenario name:**
Scenario 5, Danielle	*Scenario 4, Samantha*

First Aid

Subluxation:

1. Prevent the athlete from walking on the injured leg.
2. Monitor and treat for shock as needed and send for emergency medical assistance if it occurs.
3. Send for emergency medical assistance if the athlete has extreme pain, limited hip motion, or signs and symptoms of nerve damage or disrupted blood supply.
4. Apply ice to the injury and send the athlete to a physician.

First Aid

Grade I:

1. Rest the athlete from painful activities.
2. Apply ice.
3. Refer the athlete to a physician if symptoms and signs worsen (occur more often, especially with daily activities) or do not subside within a few days.

Grades II and III:

1. Rest the athlete from all activities.
2. Monitor and treat for shock as needed and send for emergency medical assistance if it occurs.
3. Send for emergency medical assistance if

   a. the injury was caused by a direct blow and resulted in spine deformity or tenderness directly over the spine, or

   b. the athlete has signs and symptoms of nerve damage—sharp shooting pain, numbness or tingling down one leg, leg weakness, lower extremity paralysis, or incontinence.
4. Apply ice to the injury and send the athlete to a physician (if emergency medical assistance is not sent for).

SELF-STUDY UNIT 15

Facial and Scalp Injuries

LEARNING OBJECTIVES

In this unit, you will learn

- how to identify serious face, eye, and mouth injuries;
- how to provide appropriate first aid care for face, eye, and mouth injuries;
- ways to prevent face, mouth, and eye injuries;
- how to identify and provide first aid for face and scalp lacerations; and
- how to determine when a face or scalp laceration requires medical attention.

WHAT TO READ

Read chapter 14, "Facial and Scalp Injuries," in *Sport First Aid*.

ACTIVITY 15.1

Responding to Facial and Scalp Injuries

Instructions

1. Review each of the scenarios and identify the causes, symptoms, and signs of the injury described in the scenario.

2. For each scenario, complete the following steps, using *Sport First Aid* as a reference:

a. In the Causes, Symptoms, and Signs table on page 199, find the column that lists information for the injury described in the scenario. Write the injury name and scenario name (e.g., "Scenario 2, Lee") at the top of the appropriate column.

b. In the First Aid table on page 200, find the column that shows the steps to take for the injury described in the scenario, and write the injury name and scenario name at the top of the appropriate column.

▶ *Scenario 1, John* -

John is fielding when he misses a pop fly and it hits him squarely in the eye. You pull him out of the game to check his injury. At first John denies any problem, but after a few minutes, he admits that his vision is blurred or doubled; he's not sure which. You can see a little blood pooling in the white of his eye. You don't see any obvious deformity or sunkenness. You get out your penlight to check John's pupils, and John has trouble keeping his eye open when you shine the light in his injured eye.

▶ *Scenario 2, Lee* -

Lee arrives at ice hockey practice late. He skates onto the ice and is about to pull his mask down when an airborne puck hits him in the face. Lee immediately grimaces in pain. You walk over to check his injury. Lee tells you that the puck hit him in the nose, and you can see that his nose is beginning to swell and bruise. A small amount of blood is draining from Lee's nose. You ask Lee how his vision is, and he says it's fine, but he adds that he can't breathe very well through his nose. The bridge of Lee's nose looks crooked.

▶ *Scenario 3, Tori* -

Tori and Lexie are playing doubles tennis when they miscommunicate about a ball coming down the middle, and Lexie's racket hits Tori just above her eye. As Tori runs to you on the sidelines, you can see a lot of blood coming from the wound. Tori is scared by the large amount of blood, but you quickly sit her down, reassure her, and give her a towel to hold against the wound. You put on a pair of examination gloves and take a closer look. You see a deep cut above Tori's eyebrow, but the edges of the wound are touching. The area is swelling a little, but you don't see any other obvious deformity. Tori's vision is fine, and her pupils are equal and reactive. You gently touch the area around both eyes, and the bone structure seems intact and similar for both eyes.

▶ Scenario 4, Josh -

Josh gets elbowed hard in the mouth during a basketball game. He stops where he is on the court and actually pulls a tooth from his mouth. You run to his aid and, seeing the tooth, tell Josh not to touch the root. You send an assistant to get a container with milk and quickly put on examination gloves. You then check Josh for other injuries. He is bleeding from his mouth and is in a lot of pain. His gums are swelling where the tooth is missing, but you can see no other injuries. Josh says it's only his mouth that hurts. You carefully rinse the tooth with water, then immerse it in the container of milk. You seat Josh on the bench, telling him to lean his head forward. Next you clean Josh's bleeding tooth socket with water, then have him apply pressure with a piece of cotton for 5 minutes. Josh's breathing and circulation are normal. You motion for Josh's parents to come over, and you recommend that they go to a dentist immediately.

Causes, Symptoms, and Signs Table

Injury name: Scenario name:	Injury name: Scenario name:	Injury name: Scenario name:	Injury name: Scenario name:
Cause • Direct blow or contact with an object such as a ball, elbow, or racket	**Cause** • Direct blow	**Cause** • Direct blow	**Cause** • Direct blow (such as by an elbow or ball)
Symptom • Pain	**Symptoms** • Pain • Grating sensation	**Symptom** • Pain	**Symptoms** • Blind spot • Double vision • Floating spots in vision • Persistent blurred vision • Pain • Perception of flashing light
Signs • Rapid bleeding (Face and scalp lacerations tend to bleed heavily because of the extensive network of blood vessels in the area. However, they often look worse than they really are.) • Swelling • Possible bruising	**Signs** • Swelling • Discoloration • Possible deformity • Possible bleeding • Inability to breathe through the nose	**Signs** • Bleeding • Tooth totally dislodged • Swelling of gums	**Signs** • Blood pooling in white of eye or iris • Restricted eye motion • Irregularly shaped iris or pupil • Cut to the cornea • Dark tissue sticking out of cornea or sclera • Pupil inequality (reaction to light, size, tracking) • Inability to open eye • Loss of peripheral vision • Palpable defect of bones around the eye • Sensitivity to light • Pupils misaligned (one higher than other)

First Aid Table

Injury name:	Injury name:
Scenario name:	Scenario name:

First Aid	**First Aid**
1. Call for emergency medical assistance.	1. Hold the tooth by the crown, not the root. Rinse it in water (don't scrub), then immerse it in milk.
2. Seat the athlete in an upright or semireclining position (45 degrees).	2. Seat the athlete with the head forward to allow blood to drain from the mouth.
3. If emergency assistance is delayed more than 15 minutes, loosely apply an eye patch over both eyes (to limit motion).	3. Clean bleeding wounds with saline solution or tap water, then apply pressure with a piece of cotton for 5 minutes.
4. Monitor breathing and provide CPR as needed.	4. Send the athlete to a dentist immediately! The best chance for successful reimplantation of the tooth is if it is done within 30 minutes of the injury.
5. Monitor and treat for shock as needed.	5. If the athlete is experiencing breathing difficulties, shock, closed head or spine injury, compound facial fracture, or other unstable injuries,
6. Begin secondary survey.	a. send for emergency medical assistance,
	b. monitor breathing and provide CPR as needed, and
	c. monitor and treat for shock as needed.

Injury name:	Injury name:
_____	_____
Scenario name:	Scenario name:
_____	_____

First Aid	**First Aid**
1. Place the athlete in a seated position (as long as the athlete is not suffering from shock or a spine injury).	1. Seat the athlete with the head forward to allow blood and fluid to drain from the mouth.
2. Cover the injury with sterile gauze and apply pressure.	2. Gently apply ice for 15 minutes.
3. After bleeding stops, cover the injury with sterile gauze or bandage.	3. Gently pinch the nostrils shut with gauze as needed to stop bleeding.
4. Send the athlete to a physician if the edges of the wound gape apart (they don't touch), if you're unable to completely clean the wound, if debris is in the wound, or if a foreign body is embedded in the wound.	4. Send the athlete to a physician.
5. If bleeding does not stop, or athlete is experiencing breathing and circulation problems, spine or closed head injury, or other unstable or serious injuries,	
a. send for emergency medical assistance,	
b. monitor breathing and provide CPR as needed, and	
c. monitor and treat for shock as needed.	

ACTIVITY 15.1

Responding to Facial and Scalp Injuries

Causes, Symptoms, and Signs Table

Injury name: _Face and scalp laceration_ **Scenario name:** _Scenario 3, Tori_	Injury name: _Broken nose_ **Scenario name:** _Scenario 2, Lee_	Injury name: _Dislocated tooth_ **Scenario name:** _Scenario 4, Josh_	Injury name: _Eye contusion_ **Scenario name:** _Scenario 1, John_
Cause • Direct blow or contact with an object such as a ball, elbow, or racket	**Cause** • Direct blow	**Cause** • Direct blow	**Cause** • Direct blow (such as by an elbow or ball)
Symptom • Pain	**Symptoms** • Pain • Grating sensation	**Symptom** • Pain	**Symptoms** • Blind spot • Double vision • Floating spots in vision • Persistent blurred vision • Pain • Perception of flashing light
Signs • Rapid bleeding (Face and scalp lacerations tend to bleed heavily because of the extensive network of blood vessels in the area. However, they often look worse than they really are.) • Swelling • Possible bruising	**Signs** • Swelling • Discoloration • Possible deformity • Possible bleeding • Inability to breathe through the nose	**Signs** • Bleeding • Tooth totally dislodged • Swelling of gums	**Signs** • Blood pooling in white of eye or iris • Restricted eye motion • Irregularly shaped iris or pupil • Cut to the cornea • Dark tissue sticking out of cornea or sclera • Pupil inequality (reaction to light, size, tracking) • Inability to open eye • Loss of peripheral vision • Palpable defect of bones around the eye • Sensitivity to light • Pupils misaligned (one higher than other)

First Aid Table

Injury name: _Eye contusion_ Scenario name: _Scenario 1, John_	Injury name: _Dislocated tooth_ Scenario name: _Scenario 4, Josh_
First Aid 1. Call for emergency medical assistance. 2. Seat the athlete in an upright or semireclining position (45 degrees). 3. If emergency assistance is delayed more than 15 minutes, loosely apply an eye patch over both eyes (to limit motion). 4. Monitor breathing and provide CPR as needed. 5. Monitor and treat for shock as needed. 6. Begin secondary survey.	**First Aid** 1. Hold the tooth by the crown, not the root. Rinse it in water (don't scrub), then immerse it in milk. 2. Seat the athlete with the head forward to allow blood to drain from the mouth. 3. Clean bleeding wounds with saline solution or tap water, then apply pressure with a piece of cotton for 5 minutes. 4. Send the athlete to a dentist immediately! The best chance for successful reimplantation of the tooth is if it is done within 30 minutes of the injury. 5. If the athlete is experiencing breathing difficulties, shock, closed head or spine injury, compound facial fracture, or other unstable injuries, a. send for emergency medical assistance, b. monitor breathing and provide CPR as needed, and c. monitor and treat for shock as needed.

(continued)

First Aid Table *(continued)*

Injury name:	Injury name:
Face and scalp laceration	_Broken nose_
Scenario name:	**Scenario name:**
Scenario 3, Tori	_Scenario 2, Lee_
First Aid	**First Aid**
1. Place the athlete in a seated position (as long as the athlete is not suffering from shock or a spine injury).	1. Seat the athlete with the head forward to allow blood and fluid to drain from the mouth.
2. Cover the injury with sterile gauze and apply pressure.	2. Gently apply ice for 15 minutes.
3. After bleeding stops, cover the injury with sterile gauze or bandage.	3. Gently pinch the nostrils shut with gauze as needed to stop bleeding.
4. Send the athlete to a physician if the edges of the wound gape apart (they don't touch), if you're unable to completely clean the wound, if debris is in the wound, or if a foreign body is embedded in the wound.	4. Send the athlete to a physician.
5. If bleeding does not stop, or athlete is experiencing breathing and circulation problems, spine or closed head injury, or other unstable or serious injuries, a. send for emergency medical assistance, b. monitor breathing and provide CPR as needed, and c. monitor and treat for shock as needed.	

Skin Problems

LEARNING OBJECTIVES

In this unit, you will learn

- how to recognize and provide first aid care for common noncontagious skin conditions such as blisters and abrasions,
- how to recognize contagious skin conditions,
- when a skin condition requires a physician's evaluation, and
- how to prevent contagious skin conditions from spreading among athletes.

WHAT TO READ

Read chapter 15, "Skin Problems," in *Sport First Aid.*

ACTIVITY 16.1

Responding to Skin Problems

Instructions

1. Review each of the scenarios and identify the causes, symptoms, and signs of the condition described in the scenario.
2. For each scenario, complete the following steps, using *Sport First Aid* as a reference:
   a. In the Causes, Symptoms, and Signs table on page 207, find the column that lists information for the condition described in the scenario. Write the condition name and scenario name (e.g., "Scenario 2, Mandy") at the top of the appropriate column.

b. In the First Aid table on page 208, find the column that shows the steps to take for the condition described in the scenario, and write the condition name and scenario name at the top of the appropriate column.

▶ Scenario 1, Tamika -

After track practice one day, you notice that Tamika is favoring one foot. You jog up to her and ask what's the matter. She tells you that she bought new shoes and just needs to break them in. You ask Tamika where it hurts. She says that both heels hurt, but her right one hurts more than her left. When you examine her feet, you see an area of redness on the back of her left heel and torn skin and redness on the back of her right heel. Tamika complains of a burning sensation, particularly on her right heel.

▶ Scenario 2, Mandy -

Mandy hobbles off the basketball court, but you know she wasn't directly injured. You ask her what's wrong, and she says one of her toes hurts. You inspect her feet and find that one toe is swollen and red near the nail. You ask Mandy where it hurts, and she tells you the pain is near the sides of her toenail, especially when she's wearing shoes. You can see that Mandy has trimmed her toenails at an angle.

▶ Scenario 3, Tom -

Tom, who is usually pretty calm, can't seem to stand still during practice. You notice him rubbing his feet on the floor and looking generally uncomfortable. After practice, you check in on Tom and ask him about his fidgetiness. He says he can't stand the itching and burning. He shows you his feet, and you see a red, scaly rash around his toes and cracking skin on other areas of his feet.

▶ Scenario 4, Jerome -

After his shower, Jerome sheepishly approaches you in the locker room and asks if he can talk with you. He drops his towel, points to his crotch, and tells you that he has some itching and burning. He says he's never had this problem before. You can see that his skin is red and scaly.

Causes, Symptoms, and Signs Table

Condition name: _____ Scenario name: _____	Condition name: _____ Scenario name: _____	Condition name: _____ Scenario name: _____	Condition name: _____ Scenario name: _____
Cause • Friction from the skin rubbing against a surface (such as a shoe, bat, or racket handle) causes the skin layers to separate and fill with fluid	**Cause** • Prolonged exposure of the skin to a sweaty, hot environment. (An example would be rewearing soiled, damp practice clothes.)	**Cause** • Prolonged exposure of feet to a sweaty, hot, and poorly ventilated environment. (An example would be leather shoes with dirty, wet socks.)	**Causes** • Trimming nails at an angle—toward the sides • Tight shoes or socks • Toenail deformity
Symptoms • Pain • Burning • Warmth	**Symptoms** • Burning • Itching	**Symptoms** • Burning • Itching	**Symptom** • Pain on sides of toenail
Signs Closed: • Redness • Fluid-filled bump underneath the skin Open: • Torn skin • Open wound or bleeding • Redness	**Sign** • Red, scaly patches of skin	**Signs** • Red, scaly rash around the toes and other areas of the feet • Peeling or cracking skin • Blisters (severe cases)	**Signs** • Redness • Warmth • Swelling • Pus (severe)

First Aid Table

Condition name: _____ Scenario name: _____	Condition name: _____ Scenario name: _____
First Aid Instruct the athlete to do the following: 1. Frequently change socks to keep feet dry. 2. Wash and thoroughly dry feet daily. 3. Apply antifungal cream or powder to the area. 4. Go to a physician if symptoms persist.	**First Aid** Closed blisters: 1. Leave the blister intact (opening it may cause infection). 2. Adhere a commercial callus or corn pad over the blister to protect against further irritation and allow healing. 3. Instruct the athlete to keep the area clean. Open blisters: 1. Clean the area with antiseptic solution or soap. Do not use iodine. 2. Dry with sterile gauze. 3. Adhere a commercial callus or corn pad over the blister to protect against further irritation and allow healing. 4. Instruct the athlete to keep the area clean. 5. Instruct the athlete to periodically check for signs of infection— redness, swelling, and warmth that progress to red streaks extending from wound, pus, and fever. 6. Immediately refer the athlete to a physician if the above signs of infection are present or if the blister doesn't heal after one to two weeks of self-care.

Condition name:	Condition name:
_____	_____
Scenario name:	Scenario name:
_____	_____
First Aid	**First Aid**
Instruct the athlete to do the following:	Instruct the athlete to do the following:
1. Soak the foot in warm water.	1. Keep the area dry by changing wet, sweaty clothing.
2. Pack sterile cotton underneath the edge of the nail to reduce pressure against the skin. (Packing should be changed daily.)	2. Apply cream or antifungal powder to the infected area.
3. Go to a physician if signs of infection (red streaks extending from the area, fever, pus, or warmth) appear or if the cotton packing does not help after a few days.	3. See a physician if symptoms persist.

ACTIVITY 16.1

Responding to Skin Problems

Causes, Symptoms, and Signs Table

Condition name: Blisters	Condition name: Jock itch	Condition name: Athlete's foot	Condition name: Ingrown toenail
Scenario name: Scenario 1, Tamika	Scenario name: Scenario 4, Jerome	Scenario name: Scenario 3, Tom	Scenario name: Scenario 2, Mandy
Cause • Friction from the skin rubbing against a surface (such as a shoe, bat, or racket handle) causes the skin layers to separate and fill with fluid	**Cause** • Prolonged exposure of the skin to a sweaty, hot environment. (An example would be rewearing soiled, damp practice clothes.)	**Cause** • Prolonged exposure of feet to a sweaty, hot, and poorly ventilated environment. (An example would be leather shoes with dirty, wet socks.)	**Causes** • Trimming nails at an angle—toward the sides • Tight shoes or socks • Toenail deformity
Symptoms • Pain • Burning • Warmth	**Symptoms** • Burning • Itching	**Symptoms** • Burning • Itching	**Symptom** • Pain on sides of toenail
Signs Closed: • Redness • Fluid-filled bump underneath the skin Open: • Torn skin • Open wound or bleeding • Redness	**Sign** • Red, scaly patches of skin	**Signs** • Red, scaly rash around the toes and other areas of the feet • Peeling or cracking skin • Blisters (severe cases)	**Signs** • Redness • Warmth • Swelling • Pus (severe)

First Aid Table

Condition name: _Athlete's foot_	Condition name: _Blisters_
Scenario name: _Scenario 3, Tom_	Scenario name: _Scenario 1, Tamika_
First Aid Instruct the athlete to do the following: 1. Frequently change socks to keep feet dry. 2. Wash and thoroughly dry feet daily. 3. Apply antifungal cream or powder to the area. 4. Go to a physician if symptoms persist.	**First Aid** Closed blisters: 1. Leave the blister intact (opening it may cause infection). 2. Adhere a commercial callus or corn pad over the blister to protect against further irritation and allow healing. 3. Instruct the athlete to keep the area clean. Open blisters: 1. Clean the area with antiseptic solution or soap. Do not use iodine. 2. Dry with sterile gauze. 3. Adhere a commercial callus or corn pad over the blister to protect against further irritation and allow healing. 4. Instruct the athlete to keep the area clean. 5. Instruct the athlete to periodically check for signs of infection—redness, swelling, and warmth that progress to red streaks extending from wound, pus, and fever. 6. Immediately refer the athlete to a physician if the above signs of infection are present or if the blister doesn't heal after one to two weeks of self-care.

(continued)

First Aid Table *(continued)*

| Condition name:

Ingrown toenail | Condition name:

Jock itch |
|---|---|
| Scenario name:

Scenario 2, Mandy | Scenario name:

Scenario 4, Jerome |
| **First Aid**

Instruct the athlete to do the following:

1. Soak the foot in warm water.
2. Pack sterile cotton underneath the edge of the nail to reduce pressure against the skin. (Packing should be changed daily.)
3. Go to a physician if signs of infection (red streaks extending from the area, fever, pus, or warmth) appear or if the cotton packing does not help after a few days. | **First Aid**

Instruct the athlete to do the following:

1. Keep the area dry by changing wet, sweaty clothing.
2. Apply cream or antifungal powder to the infected area.
3. See a physician if symptoms persist. |

Sport First Aid
Self-Study Wrap-Up

LEARNING OBJECTIVES

In this unit, you will learn

- about completing the final step in the Sport First Aid Classroom course—taking the Sport First Aid Test.

INTRODUCTION

CONGRATULATIONS! At this point, you should have read *Sport First Aid* and completed the Sport First Aid Classroom course self-study. Now you're ready to take the Sport First Aid Test, which should take about one hour to complete. You should do fine! Just follow the simple steps below.

FIRST

- Get your *Sport First Aid* book and the Sport First Aid Classroom Test Package.
- Take these items out of the Test Package:
  - The Sport First Aid Classroom Test
  - The ASEP Test Answer Form A to record test answers
  - The Sport First Aid Test Instructions

SECOND

- In the classroom portion of this study guide, turn to Unit 9, Sport First Aid Wrap-Up, and review Activity 9.3 Testing Procedures.

- In the Sport First Aid Test Instructions, read Step 1: Determine How You Want to Take Your Sport First Aid Course Test.
- Decide how you will take the test: paper-pencil or online.

THIRD

- If you're going to take the test **ONLINE,** in the Sport First Aid Test Instructions, follow the directions in Step 2: If You Choose to Take the Online Test, and take the test. **REMINDER:** On the back page of the test instructions, you should have written or be able to find the following:
  - Your key code. The key code is the 10-digit number printed on the back page of the instructions.
  - The instructor's identification number
  - The instructor's last name
  - The organization code (if applicable)
  - The last date of course

- If you're going to take the test **PAPER-PENCIL,** in the Sport First Aid Test Instructions, follow the directions in Step 3: If You Choose to Take the Paper-Pencil Test, and take the test. **REMINDER:** The course code is on the back page of the Sport First Aid Classroom Test, it is four characters long, and it begins with BB followed by two numbers. Also, on the back page of the test instructions, you should have written or be able to find the following:
  - Your key code. The key code is the 10-digit number printed on the back page of the instructions.
  - The instructor's identification number
  - The instructor's last name
  - The organization code (if applicable)
  - The last date of course

  REMINDER: Send your completed test to ASEP. Follow the directions for "Returning Your Completed Paper-Pencil Test to ASEP" in the Sport First Aid Test Instructions.

That's it. You're done. Congratulations, and thanks for taking the Sport First Aid course!

IT STARTS WITH THE COACH

Much is expected of today's high school coach. On any given day, you may play the role of mentor, motivator, mediator, medic, psychologist, strategist, or trainer. Each requiring a separate set of skills and tactics that together make you a "coach."

The **Bronze Level** credential—offered through the ASEP Professional Coaches Education Program—is designed with all of these roles in mind. It includes courses on coaching principles, sport first aid, and sport-specific techniques and tactics, and requires CPR certification. The Bronze Level prepares you for all aspects of coaching and is a recognized and respected credential for anyone who earns it.

To enroll in any of these courses, visit the ASEP Web site at
www.ASEP.com or contact your state association.

To learn more about how you can adopt the program for your state association or organization, contact Jerry Reeder, ASEP Sales Consultant,
at **800-747-5698, ext. 2325** or e-mail **JerryR@hkusa.com**.

Developed, delivered, and supported by the American Sport Education Program, a 25-year leader in the sport education field, the ASEP Professional Coaches Education Program fulfills the coaching education requirements of more than 40 state high school associations.

American Sport Education Program

A DIVISION OF HUMAN KINETICS